SCATTERED RAYS OF LIGHT

The Incredible Survival Story of
The Kotowski Family During WW2

DOVIT YALOVIZKY
EFRAIM PEDATSUR

D1522642

Editors: Dovit Yehudit Yalovizky and Efraim Yitshak Pedatsur
Translator: Efraim Yitshak Pedatsur ("Efri")

Language editing and proofing: Anat Pedatsur Milo
Formatting and publishing: Cristina Claudia Pedatsur

ISBN: 9781705763421
efripedatsur@hotmail.com

SCATTERED RAYS *of* LIGHT

THE INCREDIBLE SURVIVAL STORY OF THE KOTOWSKI FAMILY DURING WW2

DOVIT YALOVIZKY
EFRAIM PEDATSUR

Contents

Editors' Introduction

This book is dedicated to the grandchildren, great grandchildren and the next generations of the Kotowski family.

In memory and honour of the thirty five members of our family, may they rest in peace, who were murdered in the holocaust, may God avenge their blood:

Yitshak Efraim ("Itcze") and Gitel Gustava Kotowski (nee Wilczynski); our grandfather and our grandmother, the parents of our father.

Pola and Avraham Landau and their daughter Shulamit. Pola was our father's eldest sister; Avraham Landau was her husband.

Yehudah Dov (Bear) Kotowski, our father's brother.

Nachman, Hodes, Hava, Sala, Minia with her husband and their child, Meir, his wife and their two children, Ruzia, Yakiv Duvid, Idek, Alie, Bina, Zosia, Meir, Amusz, Sala, all members of the Wilczynski family. Leizer, Genia and Leibe Sompolinski, Manes Ajman, Wolf Ajman and his two sisters, Paiseh Godzmalz and his son.

In memory and honour of our family members who survived the holocaust and are no longer with us. They carried their physical and mental pain with them throughout their lives, but in spite of this managed to live full lives. They got married, created homes, had children and brought them up with a lot of devotion, love and joy. Moreover, they taught us to appreciate all the small and beautiful things in life.

As their last will and testament, they left us the directive to pass on their story to future generations. Therefore, we bring before you the life story of our father, Yaakov Eliezer Kotowski and of his family, who were all born and raised in a "shtetl" [a small town with a large Jewish population] called Skulsk in Poland and lived there until it was occupied by the Germans, at which point their lives changed dramatically.

This book is based on the testimonies of our father and of those left by other members of our family. The testimonies of Yaakov and Hanna were written during different periods and over many years, therefore there are a few inconsistencies regarding some dates and the order of events, but this does not change the content and essence of the stories. We painstakingly wove the testimonies one into the other. Since we wanted to express the stories as told by their original narrators and in their entirety, there are a few repetitions of the same events. We added notes, in square brackets, where we saw fit. Notes in the original appear in round brackets.

Our father liked to write in the language of the Bible and to quote from holy Jewish and literary sources, but sometimes he changed the original quotes to suit his needs. Here, these quotes are expressed as he wrote them.

Many thanks and appreciation to:

Our sister Tova, who travelled specially to Rehovot, in order to take the testimony of our cousin Jopie in the summer of 2015.

Our cousin Jopie, whose important testimony added to our knowledge and provided us with information that was not known to us until recently.

Our father and our aunts Hanna and Carla, who left written testimonies. Without these they would have passed away and we would never have known or understood our family's background, their life, what they went through and where we came from.

Shlomo (Dovit's husband), for the patience and understanding that he has shown throughout the long period of our working on this book, including during numerous long phone conversations that we conducted; and for his help in improving the quality and editing of all the photos in the book.

Finally, we would like to stress the amazing and unbelievable fact, a fact which is almost beyond comprehension that the Kotowski family, which had been blessed with eight children, was lucky enough to survive the Holocaust with more than half of its members making it through alive. Most of the very few Jews who survived the inferno and returned to their hometowns and villages in Poland at the end of the war, discovered to their great dismay, that they were the sole survivors of their families and that just one or two others from their street or hometown had survived, if any. How did this happen? By whose virtue did the members of the Kotowski family survive for such a long time, against all odds and in such an impossible reality? There is no logical answer to this question. They too did not understand nor could they explain it, except to assume that a sequence of miracles had occurred. Their story is brought before you here.

Our Father's Words

"Akdamut milin, ve'sharayut shuta, avla shakilna harman u'rshuta"[Aramaic] meaning: Before I open my mouth, I shall ask for God's permission to speak.

The human being is "like a passing shadow, like a flowery bud and like a fleeting dream". Time passes so quickly; Just yesterday I was born and sitting calm and protected on mother's knees as she sang "margaritkalach" [pimpernels] by Zalman Shneur to me: "In the grove by the river, grew small and beautiful pimpernels..." (Originally in Yiddish); and it seems as if just a couple of days passed, and behold, we were led like sheep to the slaughter...

"Gvil ee'lu reki'ey, kney kol hurshata ,dyo ee'lu yamey ve'hol dmey hnishuta, dayarey ar'ah safrey ve'rashmey rashvata"[Aramaic] meaning: If all the heavens were parchment, and all the forests were reed pens, if all the seas and all the bodies of water were ink and all the world's populations were scribes and record keepers; all these would not be enough to describe everything we saw and experienced during the six years of horror encapsulated in one terrible word that strives to describe the magnitude of the atrocity: "Shoah"[holocaust] - those terrible days of bereavement and orphanhood. Woe the eyes that saw such sights, woe to the generation that had the great misfortune to live through these days of hell. "Strewn on the face of a field, they would have rejoiced had they found a grave", until their voices were silenced.

Of these things I shall pour out my heart, and because of them my soul cries; of my mother who was shot in Jozefow Bilgorajski, of my father whose soul left him through the chimney in Majdanek, Majdanek that I saw with my own eyes ;of my brother, who was shot in Dembinka, Hrubieszow; and for all those who were burnt and whose ashes were scattered to "fertilise", the green fields of Poland, those who did not get a righteous burial as befits any human being, and for those who were not burnt in the crematoriums and who were never brought to burial but their place of burial is unknown.

As the scarlet thread, the essence of my memories is woven around the magnificent past of the shtetl where my family resided, where the house in which I lived stood until the final hour. A mighty and powerful chain of events occurred around me and only the cinders remained for me after the fire. Never should I forget that this happened and is no more. As Bialik described it so well in "The city of slaughter": "Because- God called the spring and the massacre- together: "The sun was shining, the acacia was blossoming and the slaughterer slaughtered".

I remember what I promised my father, who blessed me a day before his dead body was sent into the fiery furnace of Majdanek. I see it as if it happened now; how he put his scrawny and shaking hands on my head, the flow of his boiling tears wetting my head. "If by luck or by some miracle you stay alive", he whispered to me in a cracked voice, "remember always, lest you forget, that which your eyes have seen and what the Amalekites have done to you, and speak of these events to your children, to your grandchildren, to your great grandchildren and to all the generations that come after you. And you shall speak of this when you sit in your house and when you walk the road, when you lay down to rest and when you rise" ...

Therefore, I am obligated to tell the story of our exodus from Europe, of the suffering of the Diaspora and the tragedy that the holocaust left for future generations. To remind them of the cup of sorrow that overflowed with tears that poured out like a flowing river from the eyes of those who went on their final journey of agony to oblivion. Those who used to pray three times a day: "Ve'tehezena…" ["And our eyes will look at your return to Zion with mercy"; "and you will return to your city Jerusalem with mercy and dwell in it".] However, they did not get the privilege of fulfilling the hope of their prayers. Moreover, I vow "May my right hand forget its skill if I do not remember you, if I do not consider you at the moment of my highest joy…"

"A voice is heard in the heights, mourning and great weeping, Rachel is crying for her children and refuses to be comforted, because they are no more"; with a throbbing heart, weakness of the knees and with tears in our eyes, we cry for our sacred loved ones and fulfil their command 'to remember and never to forget' the many sacrifices that were made to the Moloch. To remember and remind us of everything that happened, up until the woodcutter's hand came upon them and they were gone and will never be again. It is our obligation to remember and to remind ourselves of everything that the Amalekites did to us, may their name and memory be obliterated, and to remember the intense heat of the Germans slaughtering knife that butchered millions of Jews. Let us light an eternal candle for our loved ones, so that their pure souls may be illuminated as the radiance of the skies, and that their glorious past in the small towns, where they lived and laboured till they were deported from them with great cruelty, be remembered. There on the shores of the Goplo Lake and the Warta River they built and laboured, created culture and craftsmanship, trade and handicrafts. Their voice will be heard no more, it was silenced forever, uprooted completely; whole villages, towns and cities

And when the skies of Europe darkened and Damocles' sword hovered in the heavens, I stood and heard the echo of the studded boots of Hitler's troops marching on Poland's soil. Fear and trepidation took over the world. Every bush and every treetop swayed; "a single bird did not tweet no fowl took flight" and then everything was silent, the end was nigh and judgement day had arrived.

When I recall the crushing feet of the German troops, stepping on the stones of our streets for the first time, I see and remember days of horror and nightmares. Our fate was cruel and instead of life and the hope of good deeds, came death, destruction, a bloody storm, an entire generation's bereavement and orphanhood, Shoah. They pilloried and ridiculed us, made us subject to contempt and mockery; like a dangling limb. The Amalekites cut down the branches of the magnificent tree of our people.

From the very first day of the war I witnessed thousands of people torn to pieces, their limbs hanging from electricity and telephone wires. Mothers lying on the ground with their stomachs split open, their intestines hanging out, their children still alive, babies suckling from the nipples of their breasts, but instead of milk flowed blood, while the crows started pecking them to death. Rest in peace my slaughtered brothers and sisters, wherever your remnants may be, sleep quietly in your graves and may the clods of earth be sweet to you wherever you are. We have come from all over the country to honour your memory, to say mourners' "Kaddish" [the sanctification prayer] over your graves and to swear here before you that never again will Jews go to the slaughter. Your blood will not be cleansed and your memory will never leave our hearts. May your memory be blessed for ever and ever and may there be peace on your ashes. "Yitgadal v'yitkadash sh'meh rabba" [May His great Name grow exalted and sanctified]

Amen!

The history of the Jewish people is saturated with suffering, tears and blood throughout the years of its existence, starting from Pharaoh's time, through Haman the Wicked, the Inquisition of

Torquemada and Isabella, Khmelnitsky, Petlura and up until the mufti Haj Amin Al-Hussaini. However, in all this path of bloody suffering, persecution and murder, never in the history of the martyrdom of the Jewish people, nor in the history of any of the world's nations, has it ever reached genocide on such a scale.

With the occupation of Poland by the Nazis the heaviest blow was landed on the Jews. It was a well-planned system with elaborate technical means that had one aim alone, to annihilate the Jews of Europe. The well-oiled machine of a big country, set upon a peaceful and defenceless population: men, women, the elderly, children, toddlers and suckling infants, set to annihilate them by a variety of strange and varied means: hunger, thirst, bullets, hanging and asphyxiation.

A voice is heard in the heights, our foremother Rachel has gotten up and knocked on the graves of all those who were put to death in Europe. Wake up! Wake up! Youth of Israel, our people have perished. How many sacrifices did we bring forth to foreign altars and on the killing fields?" And no one stood up as the lion or awakened as the lion cub, and no one in the town roared. They will not awaken if not awoken by the whip and they will not rise if not by the rod". Do not eulogize, do not cry at a time like this.

And from these dark clouds a ray of sun pierced through, a hatch of light was seen; there were those who stood up and fought against the enemy with might and self-sacrifice till the end. The war in the camps and in the forests was a hopeless one and heroic stories were told by "the cinders" who survived. They did not fight to win since they had no chance, but only to save the honour of their people, who were humiliated to their very cores.

The strength of most of them did not prevail and they faded away into the pages of Jewish history. Only their memory lives on in the Book of Memories so that our children may read about the events of the darkest days in the history of the Jewish people, a history that was filled with suffering, tears and blood.

Only very few were left, those who emerged from this wave of carnage and made pains to dredge up new life from the ruins and destruction and sprout new branches from those that had been cut off.

"Devise your strategy, but it will be thwarted; propose your plan, but it will not stand; have no fear of sudden disaster or of the destruction that overtakes the wicked", for "Tzahal" - the I.D.F [Israel Defence Forces] is with us. The Amalekites will no longer dare to raise their hands upon us. Before thinking to do so, they will be wiped out. Mosh'ke will never kneel before the "Paritz" [Polish estate owner] again, and they will no longer sing "Poszedl Jojne na Wojne" [Yona Went to War] in the Polish army, ridiculing the Jewish soldiers.

We rejoice that we are the last generation of subjugation and the first to be redeemed. That we fulfilled the prophecy of Ezekiel: "The hand of the Lord was upon me...and set me in the middle of a valley, and it is full of bones...and they are very dry...so said the Lord to these bones: I will attach tendons to you and make flesh come upon you and cover you with skin. I will put breath into you, and you will come to life...they came to life and stood up on their feet - a vast army. And the Lord said unto me: Son of man, these bones are the people of Israel. They say, our bones are dried up and our hope is gone...So said the Lord: My people, I am going to open your graves and raise you up from them, I will bring you back to the land of Israel. I will put my spirit in you and you will live, and I will settle you in your own land" ... "I will gather you from all four corners of the globe, and I will carry you on eagles' wings to the land that I promised to your forefathers."

And after six years of the holocaust, a new generation that did not know the holocaust emerged and was the first to be redeemed; a generation that left the crematoriums of Auschwitz Majdanek and Sobibor behind them. A shoot sprang out of "Sh'erit Ha-Pletah" [the holocaust survivors], to these dried bones, to these skeletons; a generation of young, strong, upright men like the cedars of the Lebanon, was born. Like lion cubs, they stand guard against the waves of any enemy who seeks to destroy us, and we the people know that our lives and souls are in their hands. And when the fateful day came when they had to go to war, they brought down terror and fear on our enemies all over the Middle East. With them marched a huge army of the six million lost souls of old and young, who fought with them side by side in their ranks, and turned into a military reality. They knocked at the gates of Cairo, Damascus and Rabat-Amon, with a cry that shook the whole world: "Avenge the outpoured blood of your servants".

When the planes thundered and the guns roared, the Sphinx of Giza and the pyramids trembled, the generals of Cairo were alarmed, the rams of Damascus shivered and all the dwellers of Jordan faded away. Horror and fear fell upon them by the mighty arm of the I.D.F "and they became silent as stone".

From where the sun rises to where it sets, let the name of the I.D.F be praised;

"Swifter than eagles; stronger than lions";

And in the 'Six Days War' the I.D.F saved Israel from despair;

It strokes down the enemy, and broke and crushed its soldiers, who were as many as the grains of sand in the sea, turning them into corpses;

Tens of thousands of soldiers from four nations, all strong as steel, who came to destroy a small nation, only few in number;

Rejoice oh Israel that other nations envy your young men; Those who fell as heroes on your heights;

With pride your heroes returned home decorated with laurel wreaths, glory and victory;

Who is like you Tzahal? You who crushed all your enemies and forever banished those who hate you;

"So may all your enemies perish".

And those who fell on our borders are like flowers after the reaper's knife, without them we would not have triumphed as we did; thanks to them we are alive. For them I shall cry with a bitter heart.

With the establishment of the State of Israel, from the War of Independence and until the Six Days War, when I looked at our magnificent army, I always remembered the masses that were left in the crematoriums, and in the forced labour and death camps. They are inscribed into the chronicles of my life.

I also remember what the Jewish-German author, Lion Feuchtwanger, wrote in his book "The War of the Jews", in which he describes the life of Yosef Ben Matityahu, from his mission in Rome, through to the rebellion in the Galilee and the destruction of The Second Temple, writing: When our defeated soldiers were deported two thousand years ago by the Romans, the Romans went wild, drunk with their triumph near the Arch of Titus in Rome and shouted: Yes! Yes! "Judea capta de perdita" [Judea and Jerusalem are captives forever]. We had the privilege of seeing the

great and mighty empires of Persia, Greece and Rome disappear completely; from Pharaoh, Haman, the Inquisition, Khmelnytsky, Petliura and Hitler only a memory remains, whereas we are now shouting: Yes! Yes! You no longer exist, whereas Jerusalem lives and blossoms and will be with us forever.

Yet, if only the confines of hate could be ruptured, the necessity of sword for sword be ended and instead peace for peace preside. "And they shall beat their swords into ploughshares and their spears into pruning hooks; nations shall not lift up swords against other nations, nor shall they know war any more"; and the guns, planes and tanks will stand miserable in a remote corner and be remembered only as infamous objects, as a sign of disgrace, and will sink into the graves of oblivion."

Yaakov Eliezer Kotowski Pedatsur.

Aunt Hanna's Words

These days we talk about important and interesting subjects, discussing and recalling notable individuals, both contemporaries and people from the past. We read the Book of Ester, tell the story of the miracles that took place in ancient Egypt, and of course talk about Egypt of today. We should not be ashamed of our past. In spite of all the difficulties that are accumulating before our eyes today, in the land of Israel, we must always remember that we evolved into a free nation in our own country, along a long and difficult path.

Our soldiers are confronted with difficult problems; they stand guard day and night so that we can sleep safe in our beds. The blue and white flag of Israel flies among the other flags of the world and declares: "We are here now and will prevail forever and ever".

I do not wish to speak of distinguished poets or important inventors, but about that which exists within me and accompanies me always – about that which has been with me all along the way. I still hear the words of those who say that, those who died for "Kiddush Hashem" [martyrdom] died only because they were Jews. Yet even if they had accepted Christianity and had lived like the Marranos in Spain, this would not have changed their fate.

Not everyone had the privilege of staying alive as I did, nor did they witness such terrible things as I did, like hearing people say: "Look Hanna, Jews are peeking out at us from this soap", or "These meat cans contain pickled Jews", or "Look what a nice lampshade I received from my husband, do you know what it is made of? Of the breast skin of young Jewish women".

And when the rebellion of the Warsaw ghetto took place, German women shouted: "What a cheek those Jews have! They are shooting and abusing our soldiers!" and so on and so forth...

These subjects are known to all. I also know that people are reluctant to hear about them, as time passes, they are slowly eroding away into the depths of memory, bit by bit, since life goes on, as each of us has their own personal problems.

In a letter Erich Kastner wrote to his mother in 1945, he said: "Memories of good times are very precious, as they are the only wealth that cannot be taken or stolen". Regrettably I have bad memories, and yet my memories are very dear to me, they are engraved within me, deep into my heart and soul.

Many years have passed and whether I like it or not, the tragic memories of the fate that befell our dear parents, as well as fathers and mothers, sisters and brothers, six million of our beloved people, who were killed only because they were Jews, are coming back to haunt me. Not only did these people do no harm to anyone; on the contrary, their contribution to humanity is without measure. Distinguished poets, doctors, physicists and many others of prolific talents, virtue and skill came from their ranks.

I lived through all five and a half years of the war; from the first day, 1st September 1939, when the Germans conquered Poland, till the end of the war, 8th May 1945, when we were liberated by the Russians in Dresden, Germany. As far as that would be all of which I speak, all that I have written and everything that you can see on television or in the cinema is horrible and terrible, but the reality was tenfold worse.

The world will never know the whole truth since the people who were killed in the forests or who were buried alive cannot tell us what they experienced.

I come to you youth of Israel and ask this from you: Remember our six million brothers and sisters who were annihilated by the German Nazis and their Polish and Ukrainian collaborators. They were eradicated only because of their Judaism. You were born and brought up in the State of Israel and you are free citizens with full rights. You are our flowers and our future, guard our state. You can walk around freely brandishing the blue and white flag without any fear. In Poland when we went on a trip at Lag Ba Omer, stones were thrown at us and we often returned home injured.

We have a government, a president, a prime minister, ministers, members of the Knesset and also ambassadors all over the world. The I.D.F and the police guard us so that we can sleep quietly at night. Everything that is around you is ours. You have received the State of Israel on a silver platter. Your parents paid a high price so that this state could be established, and we paid the indescribable price of living in the Diaspora, one that cannot be put into words. Our state is a great treasure and we have to guard it. Study well, so that everyone will see that our children set an example for the whole world.

I do not want any of us to suffer or feel pain anymore; therefore, I wish everybody a good life, full of happiness. May you take advantage of every minute to be happy and to enjoy life, since life is short.

There is a song in Yiddish that translates as follows: "Applaud, applaud children, as long as you are young, since from the spring to the winter it is but a short jump".

In my home a candle is always lit and, on the table, stands a picture of all my family. The eyes in the picture look at me as if they were all still alive and it reminds me of the years of my youth in my small and faraway shtetl in Poland; Years of happiness and sadness. Should I forget these years?

This is my request: Do not forget all those who were slaughtered.

Pass on their story from generation to generation, and remember that a people lived, composed of both important Jews but also of ordinary, simple, good Jews.

I would like to finish my words with a quote from the epic poem "Pan Tadeusz", written by the famous Polish poet Adam Mickiewicz, it is said that his mother was Jewish: "And I was there with them. We drank wine and honey together. What I witnessed and lived through I have described to you here" …

I also lived together with all my loved ones and witnessed what occurred, but I did not drink wine and honey.

[Part of a speech before the W.I.Z.O women in Tel Aviv on April 1st, 1984]

Hanna Kotowski, Krzywanowski, Gonsiorowicz

Skulsk and Sompolno

Around the city of Konin there were ten "shtetls": Golina, Grodziec, Wilczyn, Zagorowa, Tuliszkow, Sompolno, Kleczow, Rychwal, Slesin and the shtetl Skulsk. This region is located between the cities of Poznan and Lodz, an area that isclose to the German border. During the tenth century A.D. the Poles established their united kingdom. In the year 966 they adopted Catholicism.

Yaakov: An old legend tells that a few years later the holy mother Maria revealed herself in Skulsk. The dogs saw her and started to yelp. To yelp in Polish is "skomlec" therefore the town was called Skomsk, after many years the name was changed to Skulsk.

Skulsk was consisted of four intersecting streets. The shtetl was surrounded by mountains, forests and three lakes, two small ones and a large lake called Goplo. The lakes were connected to each other by water channels and that is why the Germans called Skulsk "Rollensee" [between the lakes]. Further to the south the Warta River crossed the town of Konin.

The four intersecting streets consisted of two long ones and two shorter ones that crossed them. On one street only Jews lived, most of whom were shop owners. At the end of the street lived two Jewish families that were considered "nobility", as they were privileged and land owners. We lived at the other end of the street. The Poles lived on another street.

Hanna: Electricity was then but a dream in Skulsk; therefore the streets were illuminated by kerosene torches and the houses with kerosene lamps. In the evenings we liked to read books in Yiddish and Polish. We read by candlelight.

Water for our consumption was pumped from a well or fetched from a pump that was located in the centre of the town.

The water was carried using a yoke and two buckets. [The pump still exists today].

There was a custom in Skulsk that every evening the town's guard came out at the tenth hour and whistled ten times to announce to all that this was the hour. He repeated this at eleventh and twelfth hour.

Yaakov: The fields for the townspeople's cows were used as pasture fields throughout the week, except for Sundays and during the Christian festivals, then it was used as a sports field for playing football.

In the heart of the town, in the middle of the main street, near where one of the smaller streets crossed the main one, a fire station was located. The station could be seen from far and wide. Its structure was similar to that of a church. It encompassed a tower and a great hall. In the summer the hall was used for parties and shows.

Every Sunday, the Poles day of rest and during Christian festivals, the firemen came out dressed in their official uniforms, wearing copper helmets that sparkled from having been thoroughly polished. They performed exercises for show, coming down ropes from the top of the tower to the ground and doing other acrobatics. Then they came out to the sounds of their brass band and marched in threes, their flag carried gloriously at the head of their column, the firemen obeying the orders of their commander as if they were in the army.

The Firemen Commander was no other than the headmaster of our school. His deputy was a tall man with a black moustache, a well built, strong young man who was the permanent flag bearer of the fire brigade. He always marched with the same colleague next to him, a short man who also had a black moustache. They looked like Don Quixote and Sancho Panza. The tall man was good looking and serious and the short man was always happy and funny. They looked like a "Lulav and Etrog" [the ceremonial palm frond and citron]. They marched in the first group of three and led the way to the church that was situated outside the town.

The church was like an island, the lake sprawling across both its sides. It was built on a hill and around it lived the clergymen - the cream of the crop of the Poles: The priest, his deputy and their aids, the headmaster of the school and the church beadle. Only Christians lived in this area, Jews were not allowed to set foot here; they could not live here or even pass through. At the back of the large fireman's building was a tamarisk tree, and on it, with hands stretched out sat a big cross. On it were written the words: "Whoever is thirsty let him come to me and I will quench his thirst". The Jews were allowed to reach this cross, but not to go past it. [The firemen's building and the church have remained in place and are still active today].

The first Jews settled in Skulsk at the end of the eighteenth century. At the beginning of the nineteenth century Jewish settlement in Skulsk was no longer permitted because of the proximity to the German border, and only a few Jews lived there by special license.

Hanna: 120 families lived in Skulsk, among them were 40 Jewish families, the rest were Christian Poles. The Jews were mainly concentrated in one street and except for the baker, who was a Pole, all the shops and groceries belonged to Jews.

All the breadwinners were either fabric merchants, tailors or peddlers who travelled from village to village with a box on their shoulders, selling haberdashery items, shoe laces, soap, toothpaste and other "bargains". In addition, there were the grocery shop owners.

Life in the town was mundane and the arrival of a new bridegroom, who had married one of the local women, was a momentous event.

In Skulsk we had a rich cultural life, which was governed by a Zionist spirit. There was no shortage of parties and controversies that took place in the synagogue. There were "nests" of both "Hashomer Ha'Tzair" and the "Beitar" movements, and differences of opinions and arguments between them led to fights and even brawls. Therefore, they eventually each opened separate synagogues, but this too inflamed quarrels.

The youth that came of age aspired to get out of the town and move to the big city. Some of them moved to "Hakhsharah" [prep programs] or to"Kibbutzim" [collective settlements], such as the one located in Grodno, with the intention of later immigrating to the Land of Israel. In these Kibbutz/Hakhsharah programs, they worked in various disciplines, for example: sawing and wood processing, bottle production, processing skins an even in the production of scarecrows for the fields.

Yaakov: In the town there was a synagogue. The first rabbi of the synagogue was Rabbi Zelig and after him came Rabbi Leizer. The surname of the last rabbi was Beatus; he had a wife and two daughters. The rabbi and the "Shamash" [beadle] used to live in the synagogue. Near the synagogue was a "Mikveh" [a ritual bath]. We used to stroll about the surroundings of the synagogue on Saturdays and at the time of the festivals.

By the lake there was a meeting point where every Saturday and on festivals the Jewish youth would gather. Here, new acquaintances were born and relationships developed from first love affairs into weddings.

Yukev: Sompolno was a town adjacent to Skulsk. The roots of a significant number of members of our family were from Sompolno. Jews started to settle in Sompolno at the end of the eighteenth century. There too, over a certain period in the middle of the nineteenth century, there were limitations on Jewish settlement due to the proximity to the German border, but these limitations were lifted at the end of the nineteenth century.

Sompolno was a destitute place. There were no paved roads or pavements but only dusty dirt roads. The houses in the town were small, usually comprising just one floor and made of old, peeling concrete. They were without beauty or charm, inside and out.

In the houses there was no supply of running water. There was a water carrier in the town who wandered around with a yoke and buckets. He would carry the water from the well or from the river for a small fee. This water was used for drinking, cooking, house cleaning and for doing the laundry.

There wasn't enough water for bathing in, so there was a Mikveh in the town. Once a week, usually every Thursday or Friday, everybody went to the Mikveh. In all of Sompolno there was only one Mikveh, which included a few baths in which the rich people of the town would bathe, and a shallow pool where most of the town's people washed. It did not fare very well in its level of hygiene.

Just as there was no plumbing system there was also no sewage system. Each family had an outside toilet, which consisted of a small wooden hut containing a wooden seat on which we sat, beneath which there was a hole in the ground. When the hole filled up the Poles came with a horse and cart, emptied the contents of the hole and spread it over the fields as fertiliser. The smell was awful and hygiene was poor. Toilet paper was not a known product, not only in the town but even in the big city of Lodz. Old newspapers were used as toilet paper.

It should be noted that in Sompolno, contrary to the other towns, there was electricity in the houses but the streets were not illuminated at night and when evening fell, outside total darkness prevailed.

About 1150 Jews lived In Sompolno. Their main occupation was trade in cereals and other agricultural products. At the beginning of the nineteenth century the Jews of the town also started to deal in oil and brandy production, in addition to, bakers, butchers, tailors, shoemakers and locksmiths, they also provided other services. There were some peddlers who sold haberdashery items, and there were also those who were not gainfully employed but instead lived as beggars. The Jews did not have anything to do with agriculture, only the Poles worked the land.

But in spite of its external wretchedness, the town was bustling with life and Jewish culture flourished in it. The town had a choir that appeared on special occasions. (Its conductor was Abraham Wilczynski, Gitel's brother), a theatre, Zionist youth movements and a synagogue that served as an independent spiritual and social centre for the Jewish community, led by its rabbis.

Members of the Kotowski Family

Gitel Gustava Wilczynski was the daughter of Mendel and Sara (nee Szlamowicz) Wilczynski, from Sompolno. Her father was a baker who owned a bakery in Sompolno. She married Yitshak Efraim (Itcze) Kotowski, who came from a "Cohen" family [traditionally a family descendent of the Jewish priests]. Son of Yehudah Dov and Esther Kotowski from Babiak, in the Radziejow area, he was born in the forests of Poland and came from a family of wood and building material merchants, who passed on the profession from generation to generation. They got married in 1905 and established their home in the town of Skulsk, by the lake, adjacent to Sompolno. They were our grandmother and grandfather.

Yaakov: The young Itcze (Yitshak Efraim) visited Sompolno by chance. Hungry, he went into Mendel's bakery to buy some rolls and there he saw Gitel for the first time. She charmed him at first glance because of her beauty and grace and he pondered: How am I going to win over this beautiful 'Etrog'? [Citron, traditionally used as one of the four species in the Jewish festival of Sukkot], until finally an idea came to his head. He went to his father and told him that he had made a decision to learn how to be a baker at Mendel's bakery in Sompolno. His parents, Yehuda Dov and Esther, could not understand what had happened to their son, who had suddenly decided to exchange his honourable profession and position as a forest merchant to that of the inferior profession of a baker. But nothing could dissuade him from his decision. "Yitshak Efraim abandoned his parents' house, took a walking stick and a bundle of clothes which he carried over his shoulder, and left for

Sompolno, heading straight for Mendel the baker's in order to learn the profession. However, this was not for want of becoming a baker, but only so he could be close to Gitel his daughter and win her heart. This was against the will of his parents, who were not interested in this profession for their son. But 'love is as strong as death' he said and 'that which my soul has loves I shall not let out of my grip'. After two years he had mastered the baker's profession and also that which his heart desired..." By the time he had finished acquiring his profession Gitel was already head over heels in love with him. At which point Itcze introduced his "jem" to his parents and only then did they understand why, their stubborn and rebellious son, had insisted on studying "the secrets of baking." With the consent and blessing of their parents they got married and moved to live in Skulsk. There, Itcze became another link in the family chain of wood and building material merchants.

Similarly, they fulfilled their promise under the "Chuppa" [canopy at Jewish weddings], to follow the command of: "be fruitful and multiply..." God blessed her womb and every year or two she brought a new child into the world: five girls and three boys, eight children in total, like almost any other Jewish family at the time. He was kept busy working in the family trade and she, in taking care of the children".

And these are the names of their eight children and their respective year of birth:

Pola-Perla	in 1906
Aharon-Leib	in 1907
Golda-Zehava	in 1908

Yehudah-Dov (Bear)	in 1909
Ida (Jeta)	in 1910
Yaakov-Eliezer	in 1911
Carla (Kalcia)	in 1914
Hanna	in 1917

Yitshak Efraim (Itcze)

Yaakov and Hanna: In those days in the towns of Poland, wood and building material merchants were considered to be honourable and rich members of the community; members of the upper class. Grandfather Yehudah Dov, was well educated and wealthy, and Grandmother Esther also from the cream of the crop. She was fluent in several languages including French and German, as was the custom among the Polish nobility of those times. One might wonder: how she had acquired such expertise in foreign languages, the answer being that only members of the upper class in those days had the possibility to employ and finance private teachers.

Father was considered one of the most honourable people of Skulsk and the surrounding areas, and the entire town's population respected him, Jews and Christians alike. He was the Deputy Mayor of the "Gmina" [Regional Council] of Skulsk, which included: Skulsk and all the other towns and villages in this region. During festivals the head of the district would also come to the municipality. They would all leave the Gmina building in a procession, not wearing any hats. The only person who walked with a "Kippa" [Yarmulke] on his head was our father; he was the only Jew who served on the council.

He was also Head of the Committee for the Jewish Communities of Gmina Skulsk, and their prayer leader. His signature appears on documents that were signed in events that took place in the Jewish community such as weddings, births, etc. [Documents carrying his signature can still be found in the Council's archive today].

In the Jewish community he was considered the town's "elder" and served as the manager of the "Holy Society" [for burial], as a "Shofar" [ram's horn] blower in the synagogue, as an expert "Mohel" [circumciser] and as a matzos baker at Passover. During the matzos baking, two Christian women always had to be present in order to testify that there was no use of Christian blood in the baking of the matzos.

Yaakov: "In every place that you found his greatness, you also found his humility". Father was involved in community activities out of faith and not in order to get recognition for his actions. He loved mankind, was a pursuer of peace, he did not chase grandeur and did not covet honour.

Whenever God blessed a Jewish milkman or gardener in a remote village with a new born son, I knew what was about to take place as soon as I saw my father manicure his thumbnail. When I saw father sharpening his nail, I knew that this was for the "Pri'ah" [The second stage in a circumcision]. I remember the fear that fell upon me when I looked at the "Milah" [circumcision] knife. It was kept in a hidden place. Father would go into his bedroom, take out the knife from its hiding place and check it a few times. It was kept in a wallet, wrapped in bandages. He would then send me up to the loft to bring him some bore dust left by the woodworms, in a piece of paper.

He prepared his tools and poured some ether into a small bottle; he made sure that everything was clean, sterilized and ready in accordance with Jewish law. After getting ready he would set out on his journey. There were Jews who lived in remote places. They invited him to their houses and sent him a carriage, but he always objected. He preferred to make the journey on foot and it did not matter to him if it was raining or if there was a snow storm or a frost outside.

He did everything meticulously in order to keep the commandment of circumcision according to Jewish law. He cut the foreskin with his sharp knife, then performed the Pri'ah with his well sharpened nail, sucked out the blood with his mouth, washed the affected area with ether, put the bore dust on it and finally bandaged it all up. He never failed at this task, there was never a baby that suffered any disfigurement or fell sick after being circumcised by him.

Father would fast more days over the year than the days that he would eat: Every Monday and Thursday were days of

"Tahanun" [supplicatory prayer], therefore he would fast for half a day. He would also fast every "Small Day of Atonement", on the 17th of Tamuz, the day that the wall of Jerusalem was breached and of course on "Yom Kippur"[The Day of Atonement], on the 9th of Av, on the "Fast of Gedalyahu", on the 10th of Tevet and on the "Fast of Esther".

At Yehudah Dov's house [Itcze's father] the girls somewhat "strayed" from the customary righteous path. Instead of just studying "Tse'na Uree'na" in depth [a biblical book in Yiddish for Jewish women], they studied French, German and Polish, also acquiring a general education from the Polish nobility. They had a thirst for foreign literature, which was not then acceptable among the Jewish youth, definitely not amidst the Gur Hassidim. Likewise, at Yitshak Efraim's (Itcze) house, things were handled in a similar manner.

Father was a Zionist activist. He was active in "Keren Kayemet LeIsrael" [The Jewish National Fund] and "Keren Hayesod" [United Israel Appeal]. He was an authorized signatory, that is to say, responsible for money collection for the funds. Every year at "Rosh HaShanna" [the Jewish New Year], he was notified that he had been registered in their "golden book" since he had managed to collect a lot of donations. He always aspired to immigrate to the Land of Israel. He served voluntarily as Chairman of the Zionist Movement in the town and took care of all the young people's immigration to the Land of Israel. In spite of the fact that he was a Hassid of the Rabbi of Gur, he was a devoted Zionist with all his heart and soul.

Hanna: In the town there were two Zionist youth movements: "Hashomer Hatzair" and "Hechalutz". There was also a Hakhsharah group of about thirty pioneers who worked on a private farm belonging to a Jew called Israel Nasielski. They were young men who came from all over Poland to prepare themselves for life and work in the Land of Israel. His farm was located outside the town and it was called "Minuscki". The Zionist youth from the various movements used to visit the farm and spend time with the pioneers, singing and dancing. There was also a big library, where one could find books from all periods and learn about the history of the Jewish people.

Father used to invite over envoys from the Land of Israel, from the Zionist movements in Poznan and Warsaw and from the Zionist movement in London. All were housed in the family home, they ate drank and slept there. He assisted them and took care of all their needs; therefore, he was well-known in the Zionist movement all over Poland, and beyond.

Father took care of the needy in the town, sometimes using his own money, in so much as he could afford to. We had a big house and our economic situation was excellent, therefore every festival was celebrated in a manner fit for a king and many guests were invited to our house including the poor people of our town, both Jews and Poles, who were received willingly and warmly. We shared our finest food of the festival with them, and before they left each would receive some cash money as a present.

Yaakov: Father was one of a kind, second to none in kindness and generosity in his town. He gave all that he could to others. He would listen to all the cries and plights of his town's people, taking the weight of their troubles off their shoulders. When people were in distress or in trouble, they would call on him and he helped them. He aided those who had fallen and erected those who were bent over; he clothed those who were bear, fed the hungry and never rejected a plea, also giving "Matan Baseter" [giving charity in secret].

Father was a believer, a Hassid of the Rabbi of Gur, the Rabbi Avraham Mordechai Alter. This later determined the fate of the entire family.

[The elders of Skulsk of today still remember the Kotowski family.]

People say that as Itcze was a big, well-built man, boasting a formidable beard, Polish children were afraid of him. When a Polish mother wanted to frighten her child, she would threaten him that if he would not behave, she would call Itcze Kotowski. The myth of 'Itcze Kotowski' became so deep-rooted in Skulsk, that despite of the fact that for over seventy years there has been no remnant of the Kotowski family, or of any other Jews in the town, a new generation of mothers, who did not know Itcze still use this threat to keep their children in tow to this day.

Yitshak Efraim Kotowski

People also say that every day at sunset Itcze used to relax in the courtyard of his house, facing the lake, to rest from the exhausting day that had passed. Shortly afterwards, while sitting on his chair he would usually fall asleep. Polish teenagers, who were afraid of him, took delight in teasing him.

One day they decided to lift him up while he was sleeping in his chair and throw him into the lake. The two most brawny guys in the group were chosen to execute the task and the rest were to watch from afar.

The two young men approached, lifted him up in his chair and were set to carry out their scheme. But Itcze woke up and roared at them! One of the young men let go of the chair, and out of fright and panic, fainted. The second young, gripped by terror, also let go of the chair and made a run for it, hiding in the bushes. Itcze got up from his chair, shook his hand scornfully at them and returned home.

For many long minutes the young man who was hiding in the bushes was afraid to come out and he just left his friend, who was passed out, lying on the ground. Once he finally worked up the courage to leave his hiding place, he got some water for his friend who had fainted, and helped him regain consciousness.

Gitel Gustava

Yaakov and Hanna: Mother was a beautiful, graceful woman, and an excellent house keeper, she was exemplary. With the help of Haya, our housemaid from Warsaw, and her two daughters, Genya and Gandel, she took care of the house and raised her eight children with great devotion. All eight children were always clean and properly dressed when they left the house. Everybody could tell that these were the children of Gitel Kotowski. Each child had their own particular charm. The house was always clean and tidy. The smell of home-made food and baked goods often rose from the kitchen, and she was known for her delicacies for miles around.

A Prussian style of discipline was enforced in the home, this was a strict discipline. A child would not even think of going near father's "holy chair" known as the "Fater Schtul", out of respect for father, no one dared approach it, let alone sit on it. (Until Hitler's soldiers desecrated it). By seven o'clock every evening silence prevailed; all the children were already fast asleep.

Mother was an intelligent woman. In spite of the fact that she had not finished elementary school she was fluent in several languages; Yiddish, Polish, Russian, German and French. She had studied at home with private teachers, since ordinary Jews were not admitted to the good schools.

Mother always found time for herself, when she could sit peacefully and do what pleased her. Following every day of exhausting work in the home, she used to devour books and newspapers. She would read every evening till midnight, until she fell asleep with the book or newspaper in her hand. We always had all the newest books and newspapers that were published in our house. There was "Heint", a daily Zionist paper, "HaMoment", "HaZfira", the weekly journal "HaTzedek HaTov", and also "Die Welt", which was a German newspaper. On festivals and on the Sabbath, she read foreign literature, by Goethe, Schuler and Heine, in German, Russian, and French and also in Yiddish of course.

Mother was known as a person who took care of others. She was a member of the International Women's Organization W.I.Z.O. We had many good friends who often came to visit us from adjacent towns; she was an exemplary hostess and her greatest virtues were charity and charity in secret. If anyone she knew was suffering, she helped them by giving them advice or by taking action when necessary.

Mother also knew how to pamper herself, therefore every summer she would go to take mud baths in Ciechocinek.

Yaakov: In those days women did not give birth in a hospital in the big city. It was too far away and the means of transportation were inefficient, therefore they preferred to give birth at home. All of mothers' births took place at home; I can even remember when Hanna was born. Before each birth two midwives came in order to help her. By the will of God all the births passed peacefully.

[A photo copy of a document which recorded the registration of the birth of Hanna in the Town Hall Diary was discovered and given to us]:

"Number 6: Hanna Kotowska

In the town of Skulsk, on 3rd July 1917 at 10.00, a merchant named Itcze Kotowski, aged thirty-eight, who lives in the town of Skulsk, arrived. He came accompanied by two witnesses: Zelig Morgenstein, a baker aged fifty six, and Yehudah Frankel, a merchant aged forty six. He showed us a baby girl and declared that she was born in Skulsk on 2nd July of this year, at 6 o'clock in the evening, delivered by his wife Gitel Wilczynska, aged thirty- seven. The baby is called Hanna. The document was read to the father and the two witnesses". It is signed by Itcze Kotowski, the witnesses, the Rabbi and the clerk who dealt with the resident's registration office.

Pola Perla

Pola was the eldest, first born daughter of the family. One day, as was common in those days, Avraham Yehudah Landau came to Skulsk from the town of Klodawa in Poland to look for a Jewish bride. He met Pola and in the year 1931 they got married. Avraham was ten years older than Pola.

Hanna: Our parents held a huge party, fit for a king, and invited all the neighbours, both Jews and Poles. It was a magnificent party; the bridegroom's family came from Holland.

At the time of the party I was running around in the fields with my girlfriends and eventually I returned home, barefoot and wearing a dirty dress. Mother took me aside, far from the guests into a corner somewhere and scolded me: "Hanna, are you not ashamed? We are hosting a big party and you haven't been at home!" and I answered: "Mother, we are going to have another seven celebrations like this one." To my regret, there were no additional celebrations like this. This was the first and last celebration.

Jopie: After the wedding the young couple, Pola and Avraham Landau, moved to reside in Germany, in the town of Lubeck. Avraham's brother, Pinhas Philip also lived there with his wife Sara. They had two daughters: Lia and Rosa. Avraham and his brother Philip studied the production of chocolate and marzipan in Germany. Avraham also had another brother, who was the cantor in the magnificent, Great synagogue of Amsterdam. His name was Tzvi Hertz Landau. Tzvi came to Holland because he was a cantor and the synagogue in Amsterdam was looking for one. They also had another sister called Haya. She was unmarried and took care of their father, Menachem Mendel Landau, the grandfather of the family.

The brothers Avraham and Pinhas Landau were very emotionally tied to each other. Avraham was active in the "Bund" movement and was the chairman of a Jewish club that was a centre for cultural activities. In this centre they held shows, learnt Yiddish and had many others cultural activities. Contrary to him, Pinhas his brother was a communist. Despite the differences between them they shared a great love for each other and they never separated.

In 1931, a first son was born to Avraham and Pola, the first grandson born to the Kotowski family, and his name was: Yosef Shaul Landau, also known as Jopie. When Jopie was just a few months old, Hitler began to strengthen his position in Germany and started his war on the Jews.

When Avraham and his brother Pinhas understood that the situation for the Jews in Germany was becoming more severe and that it would deteriorate even further, the two families immigrated to

Holland together, with their father Menachem Mendel Landau and their aunt Haya. They lived in Amsterdam, where they opened a factory for the production of chocolate and marzipan and they were very happy there. Pola and Aunt Haya also worked in the factory- it was a family business.

Following a letter that arrived from Pola to her parents, in which she informed them that she was coming to Skulsk for a visit together with her son Jopie, Pola arrived in Skulsk in 1936, when Jopie was already five years old. This brought great joy to the Kotowski family home. Itcze took Jopie to meet all his neighbours and acquaintances, both Jewish and Polish, showing off his first born grandson. "See", he said to everyone, "this is my first grandson, the son of Pola, who is native of Skulsk." And on Friday night, when the Kiddush took place and all the family were sitting around the table, which was laden with all the best food, Itcze, who sat at the head of the table, lifted up Jopie high in his arms and said proudly: "This is the first born grandson of the Kotowski family, let everybody know."

Jopie says that this visit is engraved in his memory to this day. Jopie had freckles on his face. His aunts, Carla and Hanna, took him out to the lake next to the house and washed his face with goat's milk in the hope that his freckles would be washed off.

Obviously, this didn't happen.

Their visit was supposed to last for three weeks, but Jopie was a very mischievous boy. He wandered around grandfather Itcze's office, where he found a golden pistol in a drawer and wanted to play with it! In another incident he took sand and put it into a container of pickled cucumbers that grandmother Gitel had prepared. Therefore, their visit was cut short and after two weeks they left and returned to Holland.

First on the right is Aharon, third on the right is Yehudah, in front of him Jopie and Zefirka.

Jopie tells us that his mother Pola maintained a strictly clean and tidy house; therefore, he was not allowed to bring any friends home, so as not to dirty the house. If and when he wanted to play around, his mother would send him down to the first floor to his cousin Lia's house, which was a more open and tolerant household, where making a mess was allowed.

A sister, Shulamit Esther Landau, was born to Jopie in 1937. Gitel came for a visit to Holland in 1939, and Jopie had the privilege of meeting his grandmother again when he was eight years old.

But then the horrible war broke out and Gitel was forced to return to Poland.

Because of the war it was impossible to get out of Holland. In the end the family managed to arrange a train ticket for Gitel to Poland, in exchange for a bribe, but by the time Gitel returned to Poland the war was already at its peak.

Aharon Leib

Aharon was the first-born son. He had learnt how to prepare construction plans for wooden houses from Itcze, and he worked in the management of the family business.

In addition, he served as the treasurer of the synagogue and also volunteered to work as a fireman in the town's fire station.

Life for the Jews in Poland was hard. The Poles were anti-Semitic and harassed the Jews on every occasion. On one winter's night they set fire to Itches' wood warehouse and a big fire broke out. Aharon Leib jumped out of the windows and ran bare foot back and forth from the pump to the fire with buckets of water, in order to put out the fire. He ran from the heat to the cold, and then back to the heat again, he got soaked to the bones from the water, and as a result caught a severe cold that developed into pneumonia. Aharon was ill for a long period of time. Itcze and Gitel did all that they could so that he would recover from his illness and even sent him to various healing retreats. He spent many months in these places. But in those days, there was no penicillin, there were no antibiotics. Unfortunately, nothing helped and Aharon Leib passed away at the age of twenty eight.

At his funeral everybody walked behind the coffin from the deceased's house, to pay him last respects and went into the cemetery to bury him. Only Itcze, Yehudah and Yaakov who were "Cohanim" [considered Jewish priests] did not enter the cemetery. Instead they walked around, outside the fence of the cemetery, throughout the funeral. The Poles raised their eye brows in wonder, not understanding why the three men remained outside the fence, since they were not aware that according to Jewish law it is forbidden for Jewish priests to enter a cemetery.

Yaakov: Aharon was addicted to books. He read all the time and did all sorts of things at the same time as he was reading these books. Even when eating fish, while removing the bones from them, he continued to read, something that was considered impossible to do simultaneously. Had he not died from his illness, he would have become a great engineer, since he was considered very talented.

Aharon was engaged to our cousin Betty. An apartment was waiting for them on the second floor of the stone house, but he became ill and passed away before he got round to marrying her.

Golda Zehava

Golda worked as a seamstress when she was young. She was known as a good-hearted person, in fact too good-hearted. She always took care of everyone else, Jews and Poles alike. She was very close to her mother.

Golda married Haim Bierzwinski from Klodawa. At the wedding only Itcze, Gitel, Carla and Hanna were present. After the wedding, in 1935, the young couple immigrated to the Land of Israel. They reached Haifa and there they built their home.

Yehudah Dov (Bear)

Like his father, Yehudah Bear studied to be a baker when he was young, but ultimately worked in the family business of trading in building materials together with his brother Yaakov.

Yaakov: Like the brothers Simeon and Levi, so were we, my brother Yehudah and I. We were courageous brothers, who stood upright and erect, strong as the cedars of Lebanon.

Yehudah, a very handsome young man, was well built and had muscles of steel, with thick black veins running along his arms. If a thick thread was tied across his muscles, as soon as he flexed them the thread would be ripped off. Admirably built, he was cast like a statue of a Roman soldier sculpted by a stonemason into marble. He was the best dancer in the group, the most talented footballer in the town. No football team ever lost a game if he was playing for it; he was the only Jew in the whole county without whom no competition would ever take place. In winter he would skate on the ice, with beauty and talent second to none.

We worked together in the lumberyard at home and at the railway station. We unpacked and loaded wood, lime, cement, coal, tar and other building materials from the railway wagons onto horse-drawn carts. Exhausting work, from the morning watch to the evening prayer, from dawn until dusk, and we never got tired. As opposed to us, the Polish workers were exhausted by the end of the day.

In the summer, after work, we would jump over the fence and go straight to the lake next to our house to swim together. We nicknamed the lake "The Yeor" like the river Nile, on the banks of which the Israelites had lived when they were in Egypt. Once we got out of the water and went back onto the streets, the Poles would eye up Yehuda; the ringleaders of the town's thugs would cringe and keep their distance. The name "Yehudah -a lion cub" suited him more than anything.

Yehudah was a strong man, but he wasn't prepared to be enlisted by the Polish army. In order to avoid being recruited he went to the forests and starved himself, as did other Jews who did not want to sign up. He became underweight and when he went to the Poles recruiting office, they did not enlist him. Yehuda did not want to sacrifice himself "on foreign altars".

Ida (Jeta)

In the days of joy and wealth Ida was in charge of the flower arrangements at home, on the Sabbath and at festivals. During her adolescence she was a milliner. She was always happy and smiling.

Yaakov Eliezer

I was the youngest of the boys. I loved music. I loved to play so much that I never missed a music lesson. Even in the freezing winter, when the snow reached up to my waist, I always went to my music lessons. I played the violin, viola and trumpet and at a later stage I even became a music teacher. I also loved to swim.

One day I saw some young Poles smoking the leaves of some tree and I decided to try it too. I rolled myself a few leaves and smoked them. I was not used to smoking at all, especially not these kinds of leave. I did not know that they had a narcotic effect and I fell asleep under the tree. I did not return home and all the members of the household became very worried. They went out to look for me everywhere, until finally they found me lying under the tree, unconscious. They tried to wake me up but did not succeed. So they brought me home and put me to bed, and here too all their attempts to wake me up proved unsuccessful.

My mother and father were very worried and they did not know what to do. They called the doctor who came and checked me; he said that I had probably smoked something and that when I woke up, they should give me a lot of water to drink. I woke up after twenty four hours and was completely dehydrated. As the doctor ordered they gave me some water and after a while I recovered. They told me what had happened and asked me what I had done? To begin with I did not know what they were talking about, but later on I remembered, and my parents warned me never to do it again.

At that time there lived a young man called Mischa Brajbart, who at the time was considered a model of heroism by the Polish youth; they even sang songs about him. Mischa was a strong and muscular young man with stamina, who was not deterred by lying down on nails. He used to lie on them and then ask people to walk over and stand on him. So he wandered from village to village and performed before audiences, this was his livelihood.

One day he was wounded by one of the nails, something that happened to him from time to time, but this injury was different. He was offered treatment but he refused to accept it. He was sure that the wound would heal by itself, as it usually did since he was strong, but this wound ended up killing him.

Not all the Jews wanted to enlist into the Polish army. As opposed to them I did want to and so I joined the army, serving a full term. I was posted far away from home and for a long time I did not see my family. Since my occupation from home was construction, I was recruited in to the Engineering Corps. As part of my job I built bridges and paved roads together with the other soldiers, in order to create access roads for the army.

As a young man I was a member of the Hashomer Hatzair movement, but I did not like its ideology and so I left. At the age of twenty, after my army service, I started Hakhsharah in kibbutz "Borochov", in the city of Lodz. This was a neutral kibbutz, where I acquired skills and learnt the science of agronomy, which in due course helped me to survive.

I left kibbutz Borochov after four years of Hakhsharah, which gave me two terms of agricultural training in preparation for immigration to the Land of Israel. I was in Radomski, Bolcsczowa, Poznan and Lodz. I was trained by Shmuel Hafter Woszczina. I left the kibbutz because I had decided to immigrate to the Land of Israel, but to my deep regret I did not succeed in doing so on time. I aimed to find a way to immigrate by my own means. The kibbutz did not supply me with an immigration certificate from the Mandatory Government in Palestine, so my family bought me one with our own money. I was already all packed and ready to go, just waiting to get approval from the authorities in Poland that I could emigrate, but when I went to the Town Hall to issue a passport, war had already broken out and I was drafted as a reserve soldier into the Polish army.

I had a girlfriend, her name was Pola Gliksman, and she was also from Skulsk. We were a couple for seven years and we intended to get married, but the war changed all our plans.

Carla

Yaakov: "Carla was the most beautiful of all the girls, like a Venus with flaxen hair. Mother would work for hours weaving her hair into eight curls that were of equal length and girth, a true work of art; and she was like the shining sun, you could not look at her so as not to be blinded, always smiling and charming, a source of pride and joy to the family. Mother knotted a red lace against the evil eye around her wrist, and father always presented her with pride to honourable guests such as estate owners from the Polish nobility with whom he traded.

Dreadful screams could be heard up to the heart of the heavens whenever Carla saw Haim Nusech. Haim had lost his nose, which had frozen off, and was left with just two holes to breathe through. When on occasion he entered our house, Carla could be found hiding under the bed, as far under as possible, until he had gone.

Carla identified herself with the youth movement Hechalutz. In the year 1935 she went to Hakhsharah on a kibbutz belonging to the movement in the city of Poznan, with the aim of immigrating to the Land of Israel. This was the only way to get out of the country in those days.

In the year 1935, while she was staying on the kibbutz in Poznan, riots that had been organized by Polish students, took place. The hooligan rioters attacked the kibbutz with the intention of destroying it and injuring its members, and they succeeded.

There were about two hundred members on the kibbutz, both men and women. There were no fatalities as a result of the riots, but some people were injured, among them two young women, Carla and her best friend. They had bitten Carla badly and she was hurt. The attack left a harsh impact on the Jewish public all over Poland.

These events were covered at length by the Jewish press in Poland. Pola, who at that time was already living in Holland, read in the "Heint" newspaper that Carla had been very badly bitten by the Polish rioters and that they had threatened their victims that if they dare complain to the police they would make sure to find out who the denouncers were and that they would die by their vengeful hands. Pola and Avraham Landau understood that Carla's life was in danger and they looked for a way to smuggle her to Holland. At the time it was not simple to emigrate from Poland. They approached a renowned personality, who had influence in Holland, he testified that Carla was coming to be his housemaid and so in 1936 Carla left for Holland.

The situation in Holland was complicated. The separation from her family in Poland was very difficult for Carla, in addition to which she moved to a foreign country, whose language she did not speak, but Pola and Avraham helped her to acclimatize. She lived with them for about half a year and then she met David Lewenhoff, and in 1939 they married. There was great joy back at home. At that time our parents could not travel to the wedding. Carla called home, to Skulsk, from Holland and Itcze and Gitel congratulated them over the phone.

David and Carla had a factory for embroidery, curtains and women's clothing in Amsterdam. They were successful, their economic situation was good, they were short of nothing and they were happy.

In the summer of 1939 Carla brought Gitel over from Poland to Holland. There Gitel also met with the Landau family, including the two grandchildren Jopie and Shulamit, and the young Lewenhoff family. They rejoiced and Gitel was pleased to see that they were all living happily. During the time that Gitel was staying in Amsterdam, on 1st September 1939, war broke out and the Germans invaded

Poland. Gitel was in a hurry to get home, to be together with the rest of her family.

Hanna

I was the youngest of the children and the only one who had the privilege of studying for seven years in school. I learnt to play music and also sang in a choir. I liked to read books in Yiddish and Polish, by candlelight. My childhood was happy in spite of the anti- Semitism and the harassment of the Jews by the Poles.

I read all the letters from our Uncle Avraham Wilczynski, who lived in Haifa. We the young people had hope that our dream to immigrate to the Land of Israel would come true one day; therefore I joined the Hashomer Hatzair movement. Regrettably things went in other directions. I could never have imagined that I would have to start my life anew thirteen times over in order to survive. It was an on-going daily war, and if anybody had asked me, I doubt if I could assert that this was in fact my life.

I had a boyfriend, Shulem Frankel, and I was supposed to marry him. He was a very clever guy who gave lectures and I learnt how to be streetwise from him, which helped me a lot in life. But the war separated us.

Shulem's father, Yehudah Frankel, was a great scholar and was a close associate of Dr. Theodor Binyamin Zeev Herzl's. He travelled to the first Zionist congress that took place in Basel in Switzerland. In 1917, after the Balfour declaration, he stood on a stage in the synagogue in our town, with a Herzl-style beard, which was customary among the Zionists, and quoted the prophecy of the prophet Ezekiel about the dry bones.

Sitting at the bottom: Hanna with Zefirka. Right to left. Sitting: Yehudah,
Gitel and Aharon. Standing: Ida, Golda, Yaakov and Carla.

Pola and Avraham with their children Yoseph (Jopie) and Shulamit

Hashomer Ha'Tzair branch in Skulsk: Hanna, sitting at the bottom in the middle. Carla, sitting above her. Aharon, standing above her on the left. Yaakov, third from Aharon's left, wearing Skulsk's Fire Brigade's orchestra uniform. Yehudah is standing third from the right from Aharon. Ida is standing at the top left, and second from the right is Gabrisz.

Hanna and Ida on the street in Skulsk

Hanna and Golda in the garden of the house in Skulsk

The Family Home

Yaakov and Hanna: Father purchased a big plot of land in Skulsk that was located on the outskirts of the town. He built a wooden house on it, where the family lived and also two warehouses for timber. At the time there was a law in Poland that stated that lumberyards such as these could only be located on the borders of the town streets and not in densely populated areas, in order to prevent fire hazard. In those days not only were the houses made of wood but their roofs were all covered in reed or straw and it was dangerous. Fires occurred quite often, and if one house caught fire the whole street could burn down. For this reason, our house was located on the outskirts of the town, so that if God forbid a fire broke out in one of the warehouses it would not harm the adjacent houses. Consequently, father also used to donate and invest in the town's fire station.

In the wooden house there were four rooms, a kitchen and an additional room which had a roof that could be opened. This room served as the "Sukkah" at "Sukkot" [The Feast of the Tabernacles]. At the entrance to the house there was a large veranda and a long corridor that led to the dining room. On both sides of the house there were ornamental gardens with flowers that bloomed almost all summer long, they included roses and other types of flowers. The entire house was covered in wild vines. Next to the house there was a large vegetable garden, and we also had an orchard full of fruit trees.

A barbed wire fence as well as acacia trees and purple lilac flowers surrounded the house and yard; when they bloomed, especially in the months of May, June and July, their pungent, intoxicating odours reached far and wide.

In the garden "winter vegetation" was also grown. In winter, when everything was covered in snow, before the Sabbath we used to go out into the garden, dig beneath the snow and collect some greenery for decorating the dining table. It decorated the spotless white table cloth every Saturday throughout the Sabbath. It was designated only for decorating the table and it bloomed all year round, fresh and full of life.

Mother was the one who worked hard cultivating and keeping an eye on everything that grew in the garden. Father used to go out into the garden every morning to breathe in the fresh air and pick fruit and vegetables from the garden according to the season: radishes, beetroot, grapes, strawberries and other produce. The seedlings were bought in from a town called Zlasczcyki, which was located in southern Poland on the border with Romania.

The house was exemplary, it was always clean and tidy and the wooden floors always shined.

An additional house was built at a later stage. The second house was made of stone and had two floors. On the ground floor were the warehouses and above them, on the second floor, was a four-bedroom apartment. This apartment was to be Aharon Leib's, who was already engaged to Betty.

The timber in the warehouses was designated for construction and for carpentry. Itcze and his sons planned and built timber houses. They helped the farmers in the area to plan and build their houses and supplied them with all the building materials they needed.

There were only three telephones in the town, one in the town hall, one in the post office and the third one was in our house. Father needed the telephone in order to communicate with all the goods suppliers from all over Poland with whom he had commercial relations.

At the entrance to the timber warehouse there was a large wooden board which read: "Warehouse for building materials and timber, owned by Itcze Kotowski, telephone number 19".

Hanna: Father and my brothers worked in the warehouse. They were construction contractors. My brother Aharon Leib prepared the plans for constructing houses. He had learnt the profession from father, and my brothers Yehudah and Yaakov Eliezer helped with the actual execution of the plans. They carried timber, sacks of cement, lime and coal on their backs, and helped to transport them from place to place.

About three kilometres from Skulsk there was a railway station called Krzywe Kolano. All the materials for the warehouse arrived at this station by train. The street that we lived on was the shortest in Skulsk, and when a carriage with goods arrived, it reached all the way from one end of the street to the other.

Yaakov: In winter father used to buy forest plots for cutting down trees, which he was later obligated to replant in order to replace those he had cut down. The trees were taken to the sawmill and cut into timber boards, and this was how the family made a living. Business flourished and made everyone a good living, so there was no shortage at home.

During tree cutting season in the winter, father used to leave for the forest for the entire day after "Shacharit" [the Morning Prayer service], armed with a loaf of bread, a few hard-boiled eggs and a bottle of vodka. He returned home towards "Maariv" [the evening prayer service]. He left when the temperature outside was 20-25 degrees below zero; very cold weather indeed. When he returned home his moustache and beard looked like they had turned into blocks of ice from the frost outside. It was so cold you could see his breath. Whilst mother heated up his dinner, he recited the Maariv prayer.

On occasion a loud thud was suddenly heard, it was as if a stone had fallen to the ground. It was in fact a chunk of ice that had dropped off father's beard; it fell to the floor and melted. To her great dismay, mother was forced to wipe up all the water with a rag, and only after this did, she serve him his meal.

The house was a meeting place for the Jewish community elders and for Zionists. We drank up their words and had a thirst for their knowledge. When they stayed with us as our guests we sat at their feet while they gave their lectures. This took place a few times every week. Our home was always open and respected everyone, reflecting the phrase: "All who are hungry come and eat; All who are needy come and celebrate Passover", not only Jews, but Christians too.

Father invited envoys from the Land of Israel, and also from the Zionist movement in Warsaw. All were hosted in our house. They ate, drank and slept in our house. There were also other envoys, from the Zionist movement in London and from the city of Poznan in Poland, all who came to our house. Father served them and took care of all their needs; therefore, he was well-known in the Zionist movement in Poland and beyond.

Any emissary who arrived in Poland from the Land of Israel, representing Keren Kayemet LeIsrael or Keren Hayesod, was sent from Warsaw to our home. We had a special room for hosting them graciously at the house and they were given food fit for a king. When an envoy arrived, there was always a celebration at home and we were delighted to touch any Jew that had come from the Land of Israel.

I remember a particular emissary, Mr. Kaganowicz, who came to our home from the Land of Israel. He was a lecturer. A very good-looking Jew who sported a black beard in the same style as Herzl, as was customary in those days. He looked like an Assyrian. I was afraid to look at him out of respect. It was hard to refuse a Jew like him and say: "I am wanting and I cannot give..."

When he went up on stage in the synagogue on Saturday, he

preached for four hours without a break. He described the bloody events in Kishinev. The synagogue's congregation looked as if it was "Tisha B'Av" [an annual fast in Judaism, which commemorates the anniversary of the destruction of the First Temple by the Babylonians and the Second Temple by the Romans in Jerusalem]. Children and old people cried, not to mention the women.

When the Sabbath went out, father, the signatory and the chairman of Keren Kayemet and Keren Hayesod, got the people to sign promissory notes. Nobody objected to whatever he asked for. Even people of little means donated beyond what they could, in order to fulfil the custom of "do not forsake your community".

At five o'clock in the morning, when we were all still fast asleep, father was already out and about. He brought home the freshest butter that the farmers had just brought to sell in the town. It had been made just two hours before and was packed in horseradish leaves; it was still wet from the water. The butter smelt like almonds and of the fields. He also brought home fresh eggs and other produce. Similarly, he brought us fresh meat bought from Julek Horn the butcher. He always bought the nicest and best cuts.

Father had commercial relations with the Paritzs. He always asked them if they had any meat for sale; veal, beef or some nice mutton ready for the slaughter. If they said yes, he advised Julek the butcher immediately. Then Julek would jump on his wagon with his son Avremel, and together they would present themselves before the Paritz, and in a high pitched voice he would serenade him; after kissing the hand of the Paritz he would kneel down and bow, taking off his hat and touching it to the ground and would say: "Here I am. Your devoted servant Julek is at your disposal. Mr. Itcze Kotowski sent me to you. Is your honour, your eminence, prepared to sell me some merchandise?" After such a serenade, sung by the voice of a nightingale, the Paritz, with a smile on his face, "did him a favour" and sold him whatever father wanted to buy, but always at an excessive price.

Julek had no choice but to buy. After the slaughter, when father came to buy the meat, Julek would say to him:" Rabbi Itcze all the shop is at your disposal, take whatever you want free of charge. You don't need to pay for anything". Father paid him of course. The rest of the Jews also paid him. There was no other choice. Julek was the only butcher in the town.

After purchasing the meat father would return home with all the good merchandise he had bought and after doing all the shopping father would go to the synagogue, with his "Tallit" [prayer shawl] tucked under his arm; "First the flour and then the Torah".

Haya, the house maid, slept in the kitchen. The bed which served her at night was used as a table during the day. It was in fact a board that could be lifted up, and beneath which a linen case was locked with a bolt during the day. All the food was prepared on this board during the day, the ironing was done here and anything else that needed to be done.

Haya woke up early every morning and lit the stove using firewood, later she would go outside to fetch water from the well that was located at the entrance to the property using tin cans, and then she would start to prepare breakfast. By the time mother woke up everything was almost ready.

Mother would wake the children up. In the children's bedroom there was a table and each child had their own chair with a backrest. In the evenings, each child would lay out their own clothes in an orderly manner, one next to the other according to their age, in an exemplary fashion, and their shoes would be tucked under their chair. It was like in the army. Their clothes were arranged like this so that even in the dark each child would be able to find their own clothes without searching for them.

In the mornings, Miszeh the woodcutter, used to stand by the gate ready and waiting like a soldier with an axe over his shoulder. He was ready to take out all his energy and anger on the iron hard tree roots and on the oak and pine trees. He would cut down the trees and later they were sent to the sawmill to be cut into boards. Some of the pieces that he removed from the soil with great effort, he would then cut into smaller pieces, which could then fit into the stove for heating the house in the winter.

The skin on Miszeh's hands would crack from the cold and the damp, from his exhausting work in the rain and the snow. Luckily, my merciful sister Golda was at hand, even when she saw a fly fall off a tree, she would be concerned that it might break its neck. Every day when Miszeh finished his work she would call him into the kitchen and soak his hands in hot water with soda powder in it in order to ease his wounds. She spread vaseline or glycerine on them and bandaged them up. Miszeh used to bow his head towards her, removing his hat and lowering it to the ground out of respect for her, and after kissing her hands he left for home.

At six o'clock in the morning our cousin Moishe Biderko who lived next to us arrived, erect and serious like a tree. He took the keys and opened the main gate. There the carpenters and the Paritzs and their workers were already waiting to choose the goods that they needed according to their lists: boards, cement, lime, tar, nails and other building materials. My brother, our workers and I would start to unload and arrange the goods that were left over from the day before, each wood board according to its size, category and thickness, as well as the rest of the goods. Afterwards, Moishe would open up the office and he, my father and my eldest brother Aharon went in to start the trade.

At the same time carts full of boards and tins full of tar and lime arrived. Our tradesmen, the carpenters, tar-workers, builders and the plasterers: Szmilkowicz, Szmiczul and Boicyn, all stood and waited for orders of where to start working. The noise and hubbub were like a bee hive. Then Avigdor the pauper would arrive. Not only was he not very smart, he was also a complete nutcase. Mother would take him in to have breakfast out of pity. When he ate mother used to ask him; "How are you? Do you have any news?" and he would reply: "Didn't you hear? The Rabbi's wife fell into the well". "Really??" mother would reply in fear. Afterwards he got to do some work in the yard.

Sitting: Right to left: Ida, Gitel Golda. Standing: Hanna, Yaakov (third), Betty (fifth), Aharon (seventh), Carla, Haya (the house maid with her two daughters) and Yehudah on the top left.

Everyday Life, Friday Nights & Festivals

Hanna: Every day at lunch the table was covered in a white table cloth and cutlery was laid out for each member of the family. Ida always took care to have flowers on the table. If by chance some neighbour came into our house around this time and asked: "Mrs. Kotowski, do you have guests for lunch today?" mother would answer, "Yes, my husband and the children".

Yaakov: Starting on Thursdays every week the girls would start to work hard preparing the house for the Sabbath. They scrubbed the floor using brushes while on their knees. The floor was painted red and coated with wax. They rubbed the floor until it shined like a mirror and it was so smooth that there was danger of slipping.

On Friday nights father used to go with us, the sons, to the synagogue to pray. When we returned, we would say the blessing: "Come bride, come Sabbath oh Queen", and we would then all sit around the long table, which was covered in a white tablecloth and decorated with flowers and greenery, five daughters and three sons.

When Aharon was alive, our cousin Betty, who was his fiancée, also used to sit with us at our table. Following his death, Betty left for South America. Her sister Ella remained in Poland by herself since she had lost both her parents. My parents adopted her and she too used to sit with us at our table. In addition, our cousin Moishe Biderko, who worked with us in the business, also sat at our table.

At the head of the table father used to sit on his special chair, called the Fater Schtul, like a king sat on his throne. This chair was considered the divine chair of the head of family, and out of respect for father no child ever dared sit on it. To his left, we, his three sons, sat in the following order: First, Aharon Leib, his first born, symbolising father's prowess, after whom sat, Yehudah Bear, then myself, Yaakov, the youngest son of the family, followed by our cousin Moishe Biderko. We sat and awaited his regal orders. To his right, like a crown to his head, sat mother, and then their daughters in the following order: Pola, their firstborn daughter, Golda, Ida, Carla, Hanna, the youngest daughter, and at the end of the table sat our cousin Betty, all awaiting the "Kiddush" [The sanctification of the Sabbath].

A big candelabrum was always lit in the middle of the table and on either side of it flickered two Sabbath candles. On the table in front of father lay an unblemished napkin, which was white as snow and embroidered with the word "Hamotzi" [the blessing recited before eating bread], and under it was a holy treasure: two sweet loaves of "Challah" bread with raisins [the bread used on the Sabbath and festivals], which mother had baked, as this was her speciality, and whose aroma reached far and wide. They were a shiny brown colour and were covered in white poppy seeds.

The silver cup that stood shyly inside the cupboard all week long was placed in all its glory on the table in front of the Challah breads, waiting patiently for each one in their turn to drink the sweetest, high quality wine from it, which father poured from a bottle of wine that was kept especially for the Kiddush. On these occasions there was much joy and happiness for the Jewish people and their light shined bright.

After the Kiddush, when everyone had drank from the wine, our housemaid Haya, who had always lived in our house with her two daughters, came from the kitchen with her daughters and served us the Sabbath meal. First the "Gefilte Fish" [stuffed fish] were served. Their aroma had already filled the kitchen and the dining room - their delicious taste was renowned for miles - and this was followed by other cooked dishes and then cakes.

After the fish, father started the "Zemirot" [Religious songs],"Atkinu Seudata" [in Aramaic: prepare the meal] and continued with other hymns that are sung on the Sabbath eve, singing them to melodies that were passed down from his father, and his grandfather before him, from generation to generation. All of the meal's participants also joined in, like a well-trained choir, and no one was ever out of tune. In those instances, it seemed to me as if angels were floating above us and singing with us. In every corner of the house the sanctity could be felt. I remember being extremely happy.

A small bottle and a small spoon made of gold stood next to the sweet wine. This was a bottle of Schnapps, which was 96% alcohol. Only after eating the fish would father willingly give a drink to whoever wanted one, even just a taste. He warned us in advance that this was a spirit and that it was very strong. In time, we got used to it and would also take a few sips.

That it was the Sabbath eve for the Jews was felt by the entire street. The Christians stood outside their houses listening to our hymns till they were over, and then I would say the blessing: "Praised be the Lord that created me a Jew and not God forbid a Christian."

On one such Sabbath's eve when we were still children, while the adults were praying inside the synagogue I ran around outside. A large, deep pool of rain water had formed. I, still a boy, jumped from one side of the pool to the other together with my friends. Suddenly, I fell in and as I started to drown, I began screaming for help. The children ran inside to get Itcze. He rushed out and thought to himself, "What should I do? How am I going to rescue the drowning boy from the pool of water?" He then took off his tie and threw one end of it towards me, instructing me to catch it. I caught the tip of the tie and held on to it with what was left of my strength until I was pulled out of the water. I was not afraid of drowning, I was much more afraid that mother would see the white clothes that she had cleaned spotless sullied, on my return home in dirty clothes.

Hanna: On the eve of Rosh Hashanah Ida and I used to take out a big tray loaded with bunches of grapes on it and distribute them to Jewish families so that they could bless "She'hecheyanu" [a blessing recited upon the commencement of a Jewish festival].

On Yom Kippur father wore his white Kittel, blessed each of us, the children, and went to the synagogue. He spent the night at the synagogue and came home only after the blowing of the "Shofar" [ram's horn] at the end of the Yom Kippur fast.

On the festival of Sukkot, father used to sleep in the Sukkah every night over all the days of the festival, as it is written: "Ye shall dwell in huts for seven days".

On "Hanukkah" [the Festival of lights] father would light the Hanukkah Menorah candles and all the children would sit around it and sing "Maoz Tzur", [a Jewish liturgical poem]; Mother prepared "sufganiyot" [jelly doughnuts] and tasty "latkes" [potato pancakes].

When the festival of "Purim" arrived, we were always very happy. Mother used to prepare "Hamantaschen" ["Haman's Ears" pastries] and the table was laden with cakes, fruit of the season and all kinds of dried fruit: figs, dates and almonds. Nothing was forgotten and the table was always plentiful. The poor people of our town came to us disguised in fancy dress [as is the custom of the festival] and we would receive them warmly with open arms, inviting them to eat from all the best at our table. They each also received a cash gift before they left.

Yaakov: Two weeks before the festival of "Pesach" [Passover] there was already a sens that the festival had arrived; it was as if an important guest was approaching the town. On "Seder Night" [the festive meal conducted on the first night of Passover] the whole house was decorated with flowers. On the table, the unblemished tablecloth that was passed down from generation to generation, from mother to daughter, could tell some "Ginzei Nistarot" [hidden secrets]. The tablecloth was decorated with some "greenery" that I managed to dig up, out from under the snow, which was hidden there all winter.

On Seder Night father relaxed on the armchair that was situated at the head of the table, dressed in a white Kittel, adorned with a beard and a golden crown on his head; he looked like a king. On his right sat his three sons, and mother sat on his left, looking as beautiful as a queen, perfumed in scents of myrrh and frankincense; on her left sat their five daughters, all in dresses exuding the scents of jasmine and lilac. Next to them sat our cousins Betty and Moishe Biderko, and the housemaid with her two daughters.

And I, the youngest son, waited for the king's order; I waited for permission to ask the "Four Kushiyot" [the four questions]. Father responded to these and then continued the reading of the "Haggadah" [book used at the Passover Sedder], telling the story of the exodus from Egypt, until it was time for "Shema Israel" - the Morning Prayer service. Yehuda always slept straight through the reading of the Haggadah and only woke up in time for the festive meal.

Right to left: Hanna, Itcze, Yaakov, Golda, Betty, Yehudah,
Gitel, Carla and Ida

Right to left: Sitting: Itcze and Gitel. Standing: Ida, Yaakov,
Yehudah and Hanna.

Our Upbringing

Yaakov: At home we received what was known as a Prussian education, that is to say, uncompromising, strict and disciplined, including corporal punishment. It was not customary to hug and kiss. We, the sons, studied at the "Heder" [religious elementary school] from a young age as part of our Jewish education. We learnt to read and write in Hebrew, to pray and we also studied the Torah. I can't remember how many times my hands were beaten by the Rabbi, but by the end of school I knew Hebrew fluently.

On the rainy summer days, I went to the Heder barefoot and the mud reached up to my knees. I loved to play in the mud that was soft as butter.

In addition to this we all studied in the Polish elementary school, both the boys and girls. There the Jewish and Polish children studied together.

Hanna: The relations between the Jews and the Poles were not good, therefore anyone who had the possibility to do so left the town, but on the face of it life went on as usual.

In elementary school I studied together with Christian Polish children. Even there, at that time, I could already feel significant discrimination lurking in every corner. Both the teachers and the children made me feel that I was unwelcome. They humiliated me and belittled my abilities in various fields. For example, when a school play was put on, I very much wanted to participate, but in spite of the fact that I was talented and suitable they would say: "you are Jewish and we don't need you."

On the way to school the Polish boys used to throw stones at me and my other Jewish girlfriends, but because father was considered an important person in the town, among the Poles as well, and because my brothers Yehudah and Yaakov were renowned for their strength, the Polish youths were afraid of them and therefore did not bother the Kotowski family much. I personally did not suffer because of them. I felt free and safe, as opposed to other Jewish children who suffered from bullying, stone-throwing and beatings.

In the summertime I used to run about with the other Polish children, out on the soft grass, in the fields and in the adjacent forest. I used to pick black, red and blue berries and mushrooms. I also had a bicycle and I used to ride on the trails and in the wheat fields, picking flowers from which I used to make crowns for myself with which to decorate my head.

I had a kayak painted white and blue, with the words "Tel Aviv" written on it. In the summer I went rowing on the lake in it. And in the winter when the lake froze over, all of us, Jews and Poles alike, went ice-skating. I also had skis and used to go skiing with everyone.

When I finished elementary school, I wanted to continue studying; in order to do so I had to travel to a bigger town in the area. At that school, they demanded my parents pay the usual fees, plus an additional payment so that I would sit on a separate bench. This was very humiliating and for this reason my dream to continue further with my studies was shelved.

Our parents made a special effort and brought home private tutors. We always had a private teacher who taught us to read and write in Yiddish. Additional private teachers taught us, the daughters, Russian, German, Polish and also music. The girls learnt how to play the mandolin and the boys the violin. We also used to sing and were members of the school choirs.

At a certain stage, we the daughters, were sent to our uncles in Sompolno in order to learn German, since that was where the only German Gymnasium was located.

Other Family Members and Friends

The history of Gitel's family was unique. Two brothers; Mendel and Arie (Alie) Wilczynski married two sisters; Sara and Bina Salmowicz. Mendel and Sara Wilczynski had seven children: Josef-Bear, Gitel, Liba-Malka, Nachman, Abraham, Hodes and Hava. Arie and Bina Wilczynski had ten children: Sala, Abraham, Minia, Meir, Yaakov(Yukev), Gocza, Ruzia, Yakiv-Duvid, Josef and Idek.

Hanna: Joseph Bear Wilczynski: Uncle Joseph Bear was my mother's eldest brother. He immigrated to America as a bachelor at the beginning of the twentieth century. He settled in New York, there he met Sara and got married. They had four daughters and one son. His youngest daughter gave birth to Jo-Beth, who currently lives in Kibbutz Maayan Baruch in Israel. Sara worked as a seamstress and he worked very hard in his profession as a baker, progressed and established a network of sixteen bakeries. People say that he was a generous person. Although they were short of nothing at home his family always lived modestly. His children were educated according to the Jewish tradition, on giving to charity and also in secret.

Yaakov: One day we heard that Uncle Joseph Bear was coming for a visit to Poland. The house was frantic. As always for an honourable guest, mother made the house spotless and filled it with the aromas of cooked food. There was a secret hope that our guest would leave us some dollars. The hospitality towards Joseph Bear was fit for a king. At the end of his visit he thanked us and went to visit his brother Arieh (Ilie) Wilczynski in the adjacent town of Sompolno. Theirs was a poverty-stricken home and in order to assist he left his brother a substantial sum of money as a gift.

Hanna: Avraham Wilczynski: Uncle Avraham was one of my mother's brothers. He married Regina (Rivka) and they had already left Poland for the Land of Israel, then Palestine, in 1925. They lived in Haifa and had a daughter named Rachel.

Uncle Avraham sent letters and updated the family about everything that was happening in the Land of Israel. I knew about everything that was happening in the Land of Israel since I read all the letters.

It was like a dream. We lived in the hope that we too would one day leave Poland and immigrate to the Land of Israel All of us joined the pioneering youth movements and Hakhsharah as preparation towards this immigration.

In the town there was a branch of the Hechalutz youth movement and a kibbutz Hakhsharah program that young men and women went to work on, in order to learn about agriculture and prepare themselves for immigrating. We also had a branch of the Hashomer Hatzair youth movement and I belonged to it.

Hanna and Yaakov: In 1937, Uncle Avraham Wilczynski from Haifa came to visit Skulsk with his wife Regina and their daughter Rachel. We were very proud of them for having built their home in the Land of Israel. Uncle Avraham wanted to convince all of us to leave everything behind us and to immigrate to the Land of Israel. He told us about life there and it influenced father greatly. To begin with father did not agree to leave all his businesses and immigrate. But contrary to him mother was in favour of it and in the end the family decided that they would indeed immigrate to the Land of Israel.

Father planned to sell all his assets and to immigrate. He travelled to the Land of Israel's office in Warsaw to get immigration certificates for the whole family. These were issued by the British who ruled there at the time. Father arrived and saw the long queue. He called the clerk and asked him to inform them inside that Yitshak Efraim Kotowski from Skulsk was requesting to be received. Due to Father's high position, someone came out of the building and led father out of the queue. He took him straight to the person responsible for this matter, who was sitting inside.

Father received ten certificates, equal to the number of people living at the house. He returned home from Warsaw happy and cheerful and announced that everything had been arranged.

Father, who was a man of faith, was a Hassid of the Rabbi of Gur, Rabbi Avraham Mordechai Alter. He decided that before leaving Poland with his family for the Land of Israel, he would go to take leave of his Rabbi and ask for his blessing. Whenever father travelled to see the Rabbi he gave him a substantial sum of money. This was the custom among the Jewish believers at the time, and whatever the Rabbi said was what they did.

Rabbi Avraham Mordechai Alter who had visited the Land of Israel in the 1920s, listened to Father attentively and ruled that it was forbidden for him to travel and leave Poland: "Do not go to the Land of Israel, there is defilement and desecration over there, the people are sinners and heretics, they smoke on the Sabbath and eat pork. There is famine there and it will be difficult for you to get by". One way or another, the Rabbi refused to give father his blessing and he returned home mortified, tore his clothing and put earth on his head as a sign of mourning. Father proclaimed that by the ruling of the Rabbi we were not going to go to the land of Israel after all; the Rabbi had said that it was forbidden for us to go there. He tore up the certificates and heavy mourning prevailed at home. We remained in Poland and thus the fate of our family was sealed.

Before the war the Rabbi of Gur had had about 100,000 Hassidism. Some of them were very rich; they supported him economically and shared their businesses with him. Itcze was one of these people who supported him financially for years, therefor there is a hypothesis that the Rabbi did not want to lose such a precious supporter. It turns out that the Rabbi in principal did not encourage immigration to the Land of Israel since he was afraid that he would lose the Hassidim who supported him economically. Other people have also told similar stories about this.

After this event a delegation of emissaries from the "Histadrut" Labour Federation, came to Skulsk. Itcze assembled all the Jews of the town in the synagogue to listen to what they had come to say.

They proposed that the Jewish residents of Skulsk move to the Land of Israel. An argument started, some were in favour and others were against. Itcze, loyal to his Rabbi, was decisively against; to such an extent that he almost wanted to send the representatives of the Zionist Histadrut away and almost started a skirmish.

When the Germans invaded Poland, the Hassidim encouraged the Rabbi to leave. He left Poland on the last train out and later boarded a flight to the Land of Israel. The Rabbi survived, whereas most of his Hassidic audience whom he had left behind were murdered by the Nazis in the Holocaust.

Whilst Avraham Wilczynski was in Poland, his daughter Rachel spent some time with us, her cousins. Once when she was hanging out with us a group of Polish youngsters bullied her about the fact that she was Jewish. Rachel, who was a native of the Land of Israel and did not understand the meaning of anti-Semitism in Poland went up to them and gave one of them a hard slap on the face. The guy was so shocked that he did not react. We ran home and told everyone what had happened. There was fear in the household regarding the Poles reaction to this, there was concern that a pogrom would take place, but there was restraint on their part and nothing came of it.

Regina (Rivkah), Rachel and Avraham Wilczynski. 1936 Haifa

Hanna: Arieh (Ilie) and Bina Wilczynski: Uncle Ilie was another of my mother's brothers who lived in Sompolno. He was married to Bina and they had ten children. The fifth of the children was Yaakov Wilczynski, nicknamed, Yukev. He was our cousin. Yukev was two years younger than Yaakov. Yukev also enlisted into the Polish army when the time came and he was in the infantry. When the war broke out he was also recruited.

Hava Manes Ajman: Aunt Hava was one of my mother's sisters. She and her husband had two daughters and one son. They lived in Sompolno.

Ruzia and Eliezer Sompolinski: Ruzia was a cousin of my mother's. She and her husband had two daughters and they lived in Sompolno.

Nachman and Zosia Wilczynski: Uncle Nachman was my mother's brother. They had one daughter and two sons and they lived in Sompolno.

Liebe Malka Sompolinski: Aunt Liebe Malka was my mother's sister. She married David Sompolinski and they lived in Sompolno. David worked as a healer and a barber. He caught typhus from one of his sick patients and passed away at the age of thirty two. They had four daughters: Pola, Ella, Sala and Betty. Liebe Malka remarried and had a son, but she too caught typhus and passed away at the age of twenty nine. All this happened during the time of WWI. When Liebe Malka died in 1917 her parents, Sara and Mendel Wilczynski, adopted their four orphaned granddaughters: Pola aged nine, Ella aged seven, Sala aged six and Betty. However, before the outbreak of WWII Sara fell ill and passed away. After her death Mendel sold his bakery and remarried, but after some time he too passed away. At that time Pola and Sala went to live with Mendel's brother. Ella and Betty moved in with us.

At a later stage Sala moved to Montevideo, the capital of Uruguay, in South America, and there she married Asaf Freifeld. They had two daughters: Felicia and Marta. Betty had an uncle in Montevideo called Olek Sompolinski. After the death of Aharon, she also decided to move to Montevideo; there she married Mauricio Burstein and gave birth to three children: David, Marta and Mario. Pola moved to Brazil to be with relatives of her family, she fell ill and passed away in 1935. Ella remained by herself in Poland and she lived with us and we adopted her as a sister.

Ella was my age and we became good friends. She often rode her bicycle to Sompolno and I would join her. I would go to visit my grandmother and grandfather on my mother's side, Sara and Mendel Wilczynski, and at the same time I would visit many cousins and friends that I had there. During the summer vacations we used to go together to a place called Kolonia, in a village called Zakezewek, this was a holiday site near the city of Cracow.

In Sompolno Ella was introduced to our cousin Avraham Wilczynski, who was Yukev's brother, as they were of the same age. One day I came home and saw mother and the house maid Haya busying themselves in the kitchen all day long. The entire house filled with the aroma of cooked meat, fish and cakes, and the table was laid out in a manner fit for a king. A few days earlier father had been to Warsaw and had brought home some oranges, a rare item in Poland of those days, and he put them on the table too. It was a big attraction. I asked mother; what festival are we celebrating today? Mother replied, "Just you wait and see". Father invited the cantor, the Rabbi of the town and many acquaintances, both Jews and non-Jews from Sompolno. That evening, Avraham Wilczynski's parents, Aunt Bina and Uncle Ilie and all the family from Sompolno also arrived. This was to celebrate the wedding of Avraham and Ella.

Father and mother gave the young couple their bedroom for their wedding night and nine months later a daughter named Liba Malka (Lipcia), after Ella's mother, was born. When she grew up she became a wonderful singer.

Avraham was a tailor in Poland and their economic situation was not good. He left for Montevideo in Uruguay on his own and two years later Ella and their daughter joined him. There they also had a son, named David after Ella's father. Avraham worked as a tailor in Montevideo as well, but there his economic situation improved.

Itcze had two brothers and one sister:

Adolf Kotowski: Adolf immigrated to the U.S.A before the Second World War and there is no additional information about him.

Mordechai Kotowski: Uncle Mordechai married Janet and they had seven children, three daughters and four sons. They lived in Sompolno and also had a sawmill. When war broke out, they all fled to Russia, after which nothing further was heard of them. The assumption is that they were all killed.

Salka Kotowski: Aunt Salka married Leibisz Biderko. In the beginning they lived in a town called Osieciny near Wloclawek, later they came to live in Skulsk. Their house was not far from ours. They had three daughters and four sons. They used to visit us often and we had a longstanding friendship. One of the sons, Moishe Biderko, also played the violin. Moishe and my brother Yaakov liked to play together, and I used to sing. Moishe Biderko immigrated to the Land of Israel before the outbreak of the war and he was the only member of his family who survived.

Gavriel (Gabrisz) Rogorzynski: Hanna: Gabrisz was my counsellor in the Hashomer Hatzair youth movement. He was a good-looking young man. Everybody loved him dearly, and every word that came out of his mouth was sacred to the members of the youth group. He taught us the history of the Land of Israel and Israeli songs. The days and nights in Skulsk were boring and Gabrisz brought with him the spirit of love for the Land of Israel. In the small room where the nest was situated, we used to sing songs and danc e. When Gabrisz left the town and immigrated to the Land of Israel the winds of war were already in the air. We all felt abandoned in the nest, like sheep without a shepherd.

Upon his arrival in the land of Israel Gabrisz joined Kibbutz Ramat Hashofet, which was part of the Shomer Hatzair movement and he was among the pioneers who founded the kibbutz. We received letters from him in which he told us that he was working very hard. After the war, when he discovered that he was the only survivor of his family, he changed his family name to Keren.

The Kotowski and Rogorzynski families were very close to each other, like one family. The children stayed at each other's houses and felt at home, and during festivals we all spent time together.

The Dogs

Yaakov and Hanna: At home we had a small dog called "Zefir", which in translation from Russian means "a sweet" and in translation from Polish means "a light wind" or "God of the winds". We all loved this dog dearly and called it Zefirka.

In the yard we had another dog, a big, strong, frightening dog. It was a German shepherd called Burek, a name customary for a dog whose colours were grey mixed with black. Burek was better known by his nickname Rozboj, which in translation from Polish means "a robber" and connotes aggression, violence and even murder. Everybody was afraid of him. He used to guard the house at night.

Yaakov: Father had carts and horses for transporting goods from place to place. On his journeys he would take us with him, Yehudah, Yaakov and Rozboj too. Rozboj protected us from bandits who would ambush people from their hiding places in the forests.

Rozboj was kept in a big cage in the yard, since if he were allowed to run around free it would have posed a danger to people who came into the yard. The only ones who took care of him and fed him were Yehudah and Yaakov; therefore, we were the only ones he obeyed.

One day Rozboj managed to escape from his cage. He came into the kitchen and entwined himself between mother's legs, lifting her up as if she were a feather. As we heard mother's scream, Yehuda and I came running in and managed to get him under control and return him to his cage.

Yaakov: Every day, for the entire day, our front yard turned into a fair for timber traders, carpenters and tar-workers. The yard buzzed like a bee hive all day long. At night, the tumult of the carts and people fell silent. Quiet prevailed outside. The peace and silence of the night were disturbed only by our terrifying dog Rozboj, the sole king of the yard, our night watchman. All day long he slept in a corner of the yard in a closed hut. He received his portion of food twice a day, in the mornings and in the evenings, given to him either by myself or by my brother, and he did not know anybody except the two of us. Woe betide anyone who entered the yard, poor soul. If a cat came into the yard when he was released by mistake, its fate was sealed; there was no hope it would get out alive. In an instant, before it had time to think, Rozboj would have caught it by the neck, lifted it up and thrown it with force into the air, knocking the life out of it by the time it fell back down to the ground.

Rozboj's barking could be heard throughout the street and people knew that it was not a good idea to even pass by our house. Sometimes my brother and I would take Rozboj out to the Ye'or in order to wash him and he enjoyed splashing around in the water very much. Rozboj knew that he was forbidden to touch anyone unless given a direct order. Only then would he show what he could do. Below is a story, just as it happened:

My brother and I would often go to the railway station with big sums of money in order to redeem the goods that arrived for us, and we would take Rozboj with us. He would accompany us, running at our side. One morning, in the early hours, we were on our way on our bicycles and we took a shortcut through a dirt track that was overgrown with tall cereal grains, two meters high, on both its sides. Rozboj, our loyal guard dog was with us of course.

Suddenly from out of the thicket, we were attacked by two robbers. Nothing like this had ever happened to us before. These miserable losers had no idea what was in store for them. Even though we could have overcome them, we took the opportunity to give Rozboj the order: "Attack!" Rozboj did not hesitate for a moment; he pounced on the first robber like a lion on his prey and knocked him down to the ground. The robber saw that this was going to turn out badly for him and started to scream, deathly cries. Rozboj almost tore him to pieces. The second robber, who saw what was happening and understood what was to happen to him too, immediately took off, escaping by the skin of his teeth and, leaving his friend to his fate. We then gave Rozboj the order to stop and I had to stroke him for a long time to calm him down. We took the injured man to the police station; there he also gave up the name of the other assailant. From then on and ever after they both knew that it was better for them not to mess with us.

Father's Stories about the Family and the "Shtetl"

Our house was located on the banks of a small lake. I called it, the "Ye'or" [the Biblical name for the Nile]. When leaving our garden there was a path leading out to the Ye'or.

The hillsides surrounding the Ye'or were covered in groves and fruit orchards, including cherries, plums, nuts and other fruit that were not only "good for eating" but were also "pleasant to the eye". At the foot of the mountains the Ye'or rambled quietly and around it grew wild reeds. A dirt track crossed it and separated it from a second lake.

Throughout the day, fishermen in wooden boats sailed around the Ye'or using their oars and nets. They caught fish for the Jewish landlords, the Bigos brothers, to whom the lakes belonged and who employed and provided for the fishermen. The Bigos brothers were the fish wholesalers for the surrounding area, and their fish were even sold in the markets of the big city Lodz. The most substantial fishing took place in the winter, when the lakes were frozen, through holes that were drilled in the ice.

In the summer many people used to go bathing in the lake. The women would come down to wash their utensils in the lake after meals and some of them used to launder their underwear in the lake and dry them in the sun. The women would take advantage of the opportunity to go bathing naked in the lake, far from prying eyes. Those who were more modest would wrap something around their bodies to cover themselves up.

Three times a day the shepherds would bring their cattle and goats down from the pastures to the lake. Youngsters would bathe the horses in the lake.

We used to sunbathe on the mountain slopes in the blazing sun and then go skinny dipping. The lake was three kilometres wide, I used to swim from side to side across it, and bring back handfuls of cherries, picked from the orchards on the other side, to friends who couldn't swim.

There was an area designated for the boys to bathe naked in and a separate area for the girls. The girls used to go to the other side of the lake where there were reeds and natural groves constituting a wall for them to hide behind, and from where a narrow opening led straight into the lake. The place had a special name; it was called "The Bucian" [stork in Polish].

The boys and girls used to try and sneak a peek of each other naked. The boys would try to infiltrate quietly through the reeds with their boats in order to spy on the naked girls. If they succeeded sneaking in without being caught, they were victorious and would have the pleasure of seeing the girls naked. If detected by the quick eyes of the girls, their mission would have failed and they would have to quickly slip away in their boats. Screams could be heard to the heart of the heavens; and if anyone was ever caught it would sometimes end in a beating. On the other hand, the girls were also quite happy if they succeeded in sneaking a peek of the boys.

In springtime, when the snow melted, the lake would overflow and flood the meadow that was covered in hay. This was a good hiding place for big pike fish. The female pikes, whose potbellies were swollen full of eggs, would come here to lay them.

Yehudah and I would come out to the meadow armed with a

three-pronged pitchfork that was called a Roman pitchfork. We would quietly ambush the fish, catching two or three, each weighing about three kilograms, a quantity that was sufficient for mother to prepare "Gefilte Fish" from, for the Sabbath.

On Fridays after dinner and on the Sabbath, after a lunch of Gefilte Fish and Cholent, following the afternoon nap, the "Bless the Lord my Soul" psalm and the reading in "Pirkei Avot" [Ethics of the Fathers], young Jewish couples would come out to stroll around the synagogue, which was located on the main street of the town. This was where they felt at ease, since the areas where Jews could go for walks were restricted. Jews were not allowed to walk the street that led to the church or to pass the acacia with the big cross. This road led out of the town to the adjacent villages, and also into the bosom of nature - to green pastures, wheat fields and mulberry and nut trees.

Sometimes our souls yearned to reach the forest in order to pick wild nuts and forest berries. Who would not want to pick such magnificent nuts and berries which tasted of the Garden of Eden, and to eat berries with sugar on top or to prepare berry "Kreplach" [filled dumplings]? The only question was, how would we reach them and how would we pass that damned cross which stood under the acacia...? Every "Great Sabbath" before Passover, the Rabbi would deliver a long homiletic sermon before the members of the community, in which he conveyed all the important Jewish rules for Passover, and where he would also give the order not to go beyond the cross and never to pass this boundary.

No Jew dared pass the cross to reach the Garden of Eden, knowing full well that he would surely get a stone thrown at his head or eye, or that the detested Poles would break his ribs. If God forbid anyone thought of returning a blow, they knew that it would come back to them tenfold, so it was not worth it. All the Jews could only dream of reaching the forest.

The only exceptions to this rule were the two sons of Itcze

Kotowski, who was the deputy "Burmistrz" [mayor] of the town. They were privileged, since as part of his duties Itcze also helped the poor Polish residents of the town a great deal. He did for them what none of their Polish brothers wanted to do. He helped them get wood for heating and warm clothes in the winter, in the summer he helped them with food, he obtained consumer goods cheaply for them, supplied them with work for their livelihoods, and more. He was always busy helping those in need. The Poles respected him and therefore did not dare prevent him or his children from passing the acacia with the cross.

If a Polish bully dared deny us passage anywhere in the town, my brother and I would come at him with fists like iron hammers and strong flexed muscles, muscles which other Poles had felt on their bodies more than once and which consequently caused their hearts drop to their navels when only they looked at us. We beat them steadfastly, so that next time they would not even think to challenge us. Afterwards we would pass the acacia with the cross, as if it was our home ground.

We would reach the forest on our bicycles and would return with sacks full of nuts and buckets full of forest berries, taking our sisters to help us too.

My cousin Moishe Biderko and I studied music in the music school that was in an adjacent village, beyond the acacia with the cross. We were never disturbed when passing it.

Most of our recreational activities and celebrations took place during the intermediary days of the Passover and "Sukkot" festivals. These were the longest vacations, which were seven days each, and we the young ones longed for these holidays all year long.

In the firemen's building there was a big hall available for rent for performances. Twice a year shows where put on in the town, during the intermediary days of Sukkot and Passover. The plays were in Yiddish. For example, they put on: "Bar Kokhba" or "David in the

Desert" or "The Youngster of the Village". The artists came from adjacent towns like Piotrokowo, Kujawski or Klodawa. They came with their orchestras. There were about thirty actors and about thirty musicians in each troupe. And who would host them? The Kotowski Family of course. Itcze and Gitel received them with fondness and respect. The troupes would also host us in return. During the intermediary days of the following festival the Skulsk troupe would perform and would be hosted in the other towns. Sometimes this was also a blessing. The youngsters got to know each other; couples formed, and some would end up getting married.

When balls took place on Sundays in the firemen's hall, or there was a football match in the fields, not all the Jew could participate or watch, only the "privileged" ones and we were among them. As previously mentioned Yehudah always participated in the football matches, because without him the team lost and with him, they always won.

Hanna: Once a year there was a Fireman's Ball in the town. Young men and women from all the surrounding areas would come to this ball to celebrate. A raffle with prizes was held at the ball. Once I bought a ticket and won a small piglet. I took the piglet in my arms and returned home with it. Everybody wondered what the daughter of Itcze Kotowski was doing holding a small piglet in her arms.

When I reached the house, father was not at home. He had just gone to pray the prayer of "Maariv" in the synagogue. I put the piglet in the Sukkah and it screamed, probably because it was hungry. I did not know what to do. Mother said: "Wait till your father gets home; when he comes home you will get smacked". Father came home and heard the piglet's screams. He asked: "What is going on here? Are those the screeches of a pig?" At first, I said that it was not coming from our home, but eventually I had no choice but to tell him everything. Father went to a neighbour, who was a Polish butcher and told him the whole story. The butcher came to us, took the piglet away and peace returned to our home

Characters from the "Shtetl"

Yaakov: Listen my loved ones and hear my story, I shall try not to prolong my song,

Not as a camel or a donkey shall I sing, Rather I shall sing sweetly as the nightingale, I Yaakov Eliezer, may my light shine on

I was born in a large city called "Dkak", meaning: a "holy community", otherwise known as Skulsk. A place similar to Yehupitz, Pipidovka, and Boiberik or more accurately to Chelm. Our good people were all sages, all wise and all knew the Torah, but they were not familiar with Sophocles' "Antigone" or in Shakespeare's "Macbeth".

In the Shtetl there were a variety of different characters and personalities: one resembled Sancho Panza, the arms-bearer of Don Quixote, another was a tongue-tied guy, one had only one leg and another was blind in one eye, as opposed to short sighted. There was also Chaim'ke, the town's clown, who played practical jokes on people, and finally there were those who "lived in the air" and those who "lived on the ground", meaning: those who lived on the face of the earth and those who floated somewhere up above us.

Skulsk was no different from any other small town in Poland, the language, customs and traditions were passed on from generation to generation. It had: match-makers, entertainers,

wise people, those who were not so smart, down-right stupid

people, crazy people and mystics, wicked people and good people. There were people of the Jewish liturgy, such as the Rabbi, the cantor, the "Shoychet" [A person who carries out kosher slaughter of animals], the gravedigger, the burial society and the cemetery caretakers. In everyday life there were those who were privileged and there were the simple people. It was like a dramatic musical section, a hotchpotch of all sorts, and little me lived among them.

The Radiczewski Family:

In the town there lived two families of distinguished lineage, descendants of two Jewish brothers: Victor and Ludwig Radiczewski. Their houses were located on the outskirts of the street where all the Jews lived. They originally came from Germany and were estate owners. They had magnificent houses with well- kept gardens full of flowers and vegetable plots.

The Radiczewski brothers from Skulsk had two brothers in Lodz, Izidor and David Radiczewski, who owned a factory that produced silk shirts and gloves. The factory was called "Rex" and was located at 11 Lipowa Street in Lodz.

Not many people had the privilege of entering the houses of Victor or Ludwig Radiczewski. It was not possible to enter their houses other than through a corridor that led to their kitchen. We used to go there once a month in order to empty the Keren Kayemet donation boxes. In the boxes there were always 2X18 "Chai" Zloty, which was a lot of money in those days.

At Victor's house you first had to pass through a gate that was always kept closed. In order to enter you had to get permission from Dombach, the gatekeeper, who was himself only granted permission to open the gate by the Master or Lady of the house.

Opposite him lived his brother Ludwig, with his son Hania and his wife Marisha. Their big yard was surrounded by a tall stone wall.

Here too, the only one authorised to enter was the gatekeeper Ziulek, who was responsible for the yard and was also only granted permission to enter by the Master or Lady of the house.

Ziulek was also responsible for the stallion owned by the Master of the house, an Arabian race horse and the only stallion in the area. All the farmers from the surroundings came to breed their mares with the famous horse.

We also came to them once a month in order to empty the Keren Kayemet money box, and whenever we managed to enter the house we used to peep inside, taking a fleeting look at the inside of the house hoping to satisfy our curiosity.

During the Holocaust they were deported and expelled from their houses, stripped of all their possessions and assets. Izidor and David Radiewski from Lodz were among the street sweepers of the Ghetto in Lodz, and they perished there. One of the brothers Ludwig and Victor Radiewski from Skulsk perished in the Holocaust and the other one died before the war.

The Water-Carriers:

In the town there were two water-carriers and both of them were eternally single; Meir Bigos and Antuszja. Antuszja was an old maid with a beard that had grown on her face. The worry of providing a livelihood for her parents prevented her from thinking about men or other things and she never married. They always competed with each other for their livelihoods. They could both always be seen with a saddle across their shoulders and two buckets of water, one raised up and the other hanging further down. They worked from sunrise to sun- set.

Rabbi Zelig's Family:

Rabbi Zelig lived with his family in the courtyard of the synagogue. He taught us, the sons, at Heder, and his wife, Handelusza was tutor to all the daughters in our family, teaching them how to read, write and pray. When I was small, I studied with Rabbi Zelig at Heder. I remember that one day father entered the Heder in the middle of a lesson; he had come to visit me by surprise. He arrived with a pocket full of fresh green peas that he had picked from our garden and put a handful into my pocket. They were still covered in morning dew.

The firstborn son of the Rabbi and his wife was called Laizer. He looked like a shadow of a man and no woman desired him. He hoped and prayed that, like for The Messiah: "although he has been delayed, wait for him every day and eventually he will come", that similarly, one day, some spinster would come along and take him for a husband. But the weeks passed, months and years went by and no woman ever took pity on him, and he continued to wait in vain for the woman that would save him. His sister Beila got married at the age of forty to a man that was wise, but had no brains. Luck shined on his other sister, Gitel, somebody took pity on her and married her. They had three children, two sons and one daughter. One day, out of the blue, her husband disappeared and she was left, "Agunah" [A "chained" woman, bound by marriage to a husband who refuses to grant a divorce or who is missing and not proven dead], with three children. Luckily, "A Star out of Jacob" came to their younger sister, as she found herself somebody who resembled a real man, and they had a daughter.

This entire company lived in a house which consisted of just two and a half rooms, at the entrance of which stood the oven used to bake the Passover matzos for the whole holy community. Every Friday all the Jews brought covered cooking pots with Cholent in them to a central meeting place, were a fire was lit for the entire Sabbath. The cover of each cooking pot was marked with the relevant family's name. Laizer was in charge of distributing the Cholent every Sabbath and giving each family their cooking pot, but Laizer had difficulty reading. He was not well versed in capital letters. The children were the ones who came to collect the Cholent and they took home any cooking pot that they were given. Many-a-time Laizer mixed up the pots and not everyone got what they were expecting! When the cooking pots were opened at home, if a family saw that their pot had been exchanged for someone else's, first they checked to see if the exchange was in their favour. If the cooking pot that they had received was worth it they quickly polished off everything that was in it and when the rightful owner came to claim their pot, they found it empty, as if nothing unusual out of the ordinary had happened. In these cases, the whole town would go berserk and the entire Sabbath was spent quarrelling about the Cholent. This was "Oneg Shabbat" [The pleasure of the Sabbath].

The Bigos:

One of the Jewish men in Skulsk was called Chaim Bigos. His mother, Sprincza, had two sons and no husband. Her first son was the "schlemiel" Meir Bigos, who was a water-carrier and also worked as a porter to provide for his elderly mother. Her second son, Chaim, got married and lived in close proximity to his mother. Chaim Bigos was a strong man; his hands were as strong as a blacksmith's sledgehammer. He traded in the skins that the farmers would take from rabbits, heifers and wild animals. He had a weakness for women and when he went to any of the villages in the area the farmers' daughters would run from him like from a demon, as they were afraid that he would force himself on them. He was notorious for this. On the other hand, he was well-loved in the villages because he was full of mischief and he often made the villagers laugh at all his tricks.

Every Thursday there was a Farmers' Market. The village women who knew him sold Chaim eggs, butter and other goods, but while everyone else was busy with their trade, rabbi Chaim always came up with new mischievous ideas.

On one such Thursday, an old farmer came to the market with a basket full of eggs and when he saw Chaim, whom he knew, he offered to sell him the eggs. Chaim was only too happy to buy the eggs, but first asked the farmer, "How many eggs do you have there?" The farmer answered, "Thirty pieces"; "So, good my friend" said Chaim, "let's count them. Put out your arms and we'll start counting". What wouldn't the old man have done to sell his eggs...? Whatever Chaim asked him to... So, he stretched out his arms and Chaim laid the eggs, one by one, into his outstretched arms, until they were full. Then Chaim approached him, undid the old man's belt, pulled down his trousers, including his underwear

and went on his merry way, as though nothing had happened. The unfortunate old man was afraid that all the eggs would break; so he stood there, half naked in the freezing cold, holding the eggs in his arms. The peasant women who had seen the entire show panicked and started to scream loudly. They knew that only Chaim could create such a scene. The old man stood there half-naked, until another farmer took pity on him and rescued him from his predicament. The old man learned his lesson and from then on knew full well to steer clear of Chaim and what he was capable of.

When the Germans invaded the town, Chaim outsmarted them too. They didn't understand who they were dealing with. He blessed them, saying, "May all the Germans live till a hundred and twenty". The Germans happily received his ironic blessing.

Szmilze Horn:

There was also a guy called Szmilze Horn in the town. He was short in stature and short-sighted. In the evenings, when he wanted to hang up an oil lamp on a nail, he would end up trying to hang it on a fly that was resting on the wall by mistake. Obviously, the lamp fell to the ground and smashed to pieces, whereas the fly would get away laughing. When he went out in the limelight to meet his acquaintances, because of the poor lighting of the street lamps outside which were lit by kerosene, sometimes in the hours of darkness he would bump into a street pole by mistake. He would hug it and even beg its pardon, saying; "Excuse me my lady", thinking that his luck had changed, having encountered the beautiful Dulcinea and having had success with the fairer sex.

The Lotenbergs:

Another famous family in the town were Elisha and Sara Lotenberg. Sara had a soprano voice, with which she used to scream out all the curses ever invented, which no one knew where on earth she had picked up. And she had so many of them...! Then as if by magic they would all disappear and she would speak in a sweet, fine, moderate voice, sounding like a priest blessing the dead. Her husband Elisha, a schlemiel, was short in stature and wore a coat that had sleeves that were twenty centimetres longer than required. He used the sleeves to hide cigarettes, so that God forbid Sara'le wouldn't catch him smoking. If she did, woe betide him.

Sara'le had a chicken coop in her yard, and as fate would have it one of her roosters died before she had time to take it to the butcher. So she "slaughtered it" after its death and waited for a Polish acquaintance to come by, in order to sell him her bargain, the carcass.

On the same day, she caught her husband Elisha hiding a cigarette up his very long sleeves. In a fine, low, and then trill soprano voice, she started to "bless" him: "Elisha, if only you were dead like the carcass which is lying here. Why is it not you dead here instead of the rooster? At least some good will come of it, whereas from you! What good will come of you oh living carcass of mine?" Elisha "the Jewel" curled up like a hedgehog, afraid to death. When she finished her six hundred and thirteen curses and Elisha got away, luckily, without enduring a beating, he looked like a dog that had been pulled out of the cold water of the Ye'or in the middle of winter and was still alive.

Sara'le gave birth to four sons. They were Cohanim. "Of four sons the Torah spoke". The first son was called Asher. He was a good Jew, honest and a God–fearing man. He was considered to be one of the "thirty six righteous men", but when the "Cohanim's Blessing" or "Hear O Israel" were read in the synagogue, he used to shout in the loudest voice, and people would ask him: "Sir, are you hard of hearing or God forbid deaf?" The second son was called Michael. He was like his father, short and stout and he always used to gaze from his right eye to his left pocket because he was cross-eyed. The third son was called Nechemia. He was similar in form, just a little more accomplished. He had a crooked lower jaw, teeth that stuck out and eyes that were always red and teary. Last but not least was Chaim, who was really well turned out. He was our friend and was with us, in the Hashomer Hatzair movement. He was good at everything and was among the fallen from our Jewish community in the Polish army, in the war against the Germans

Outbreak of War

Yaakov: After I finished four years of Hakhsharah on Kibbutz Borochov in the city of Lodz where I was trained for life in the Land of Israel, unfortunately I did not manage to immigrate to Israel. They sent me home and I was promised that I would immigrate to Israel on "Aliya Bet" [an illegal immigration]. My suitcases and rucksacks were all packed. I was figuratively "sitting on my suitcases" and ready to go, just waiting for the exit order from the "Hechalutz Centre" in Warsaw. Every night I dreamt that I was travelling to Israel and arrived in The Promised Land. It was a sweet dream, how happy I was. I was so sorry when I woke up each morning and realised once more that it was only a dream.

This was during the period before the "Days of Awe"[the ten days of repentance between Rosh Hashanah and Yom Kippur]. At home, around the big yard, the lilac and acacia trees were blooming and their strong, intoxicating scents struck the nose of anyone who passed by in the vicinity.

I remember I was in a deep sleep and the windows were open. During the early hours, while I was in the middle of my sweet dream, I felt a strong hand suddenly take hold of me and wake me up declaring in a loud voice: "Wake up, there is a general mobilization". I got up quickly and felt as if someone had stunned me with the blow of an axe to the head. I was completely confused. I heard my mother, father and sisters all crying. Outside there was a tumult of carts and cars that were transporting soldiers from the adjacent villages to the train station. I understood that war had broken out.

Two days before I had heard the non-stop rattle of carts from afar. When I went out to the main road to see what was going on I saw that the road was full of convoys. Endless rows of farmers' carts laden with their children, wives and all their worldly possessions. The carts were loaded with the most valuable articles that they could take with them. Their cows and horses, which were tied to the carts, were being dragged behind them and chicken and geese coops were piled up next to the people sitting on the carts. The Fifth Column of the Germans, the "Volksdeutsche" [ethnic Germans who lived outside the borders of Germany, in this case Germans resident in Poland], threw flyers in the town's streets ordering the residents to leave, warning them that the front lines would pass through here since we were close to the border and a war was about to break out. The flyers instructed the residents to escape east, towards the quiet Russian border.

As soon as the war broke out, from the very first day, German planes attacked and bombarded the convoys, sowing destruction and carnage on all the roads which were crammed full of people and animals. Within ten minutes, the roads were strewn with thousands of dead corpses of human beings and livestock blood mixed with blood. The road looked as if it was covered in a bleeding mass of flesh; dismembered body parts scattered in every direction.

We embarked on a train that transported us to Poznan. By the second day we had started out on a hundred-kilometre journey on foot. We walked through the day and night, carrying all the military equipment given to us as soldiers of the Engineers Corps on our backs. Each of us carried about sixty kilograms. By the time we reached our destination, the bank of the Warta River near Konin, we were completely exhausted. We took the equipment off our shoulders; our bodies were covered in black stripes from the belts, where the blood had stopped flowing.

We built a bridge from one side of the river to the other side. When we finally finished, we passed over it towards the front. There, I, and many of my Jewish friends from our region, engaged in blood-soaked battles. Rivers of blood poured in Kutno and Lenczyca, it was a war fought with bayonets, the territory passed from hand to hand, and it was a face to face war, but not of equal means and forces. During the day German planes bombarded us and at night we endured heavy barrages of artillery. All this quickly defeated the Polish army.

On the fourth day I was completely exhausted, I had been in battle all day, every day, without any food or water. The battle had already been determined. The German army had already moved passed us, and all the civilians had escaped eastwards. There was not a soul left in the surrounding area. All around us were only burnt down villages and the remnants of destroyed roads and bridges. In this state I walked around looking for food and water. I could not find anything.

I reached a village that had been burnt down and saw a carpentry shop that was half burnt; its door was partially open. I went inside in the hope that I might find food or water, but alas, no. Inside lay dead people and injured people on the verge of death who were begging for help. I was completely exhausted and desperate, I lay down among them and said to myself; let me lie among them and await my death; "the ropes of death tightening their grip on me"; that was when "I called upon Jah in my distress" and at that time: "You lifted me up from the grave. You kept me alive; you spared me from sinking into the pit."

I was lying and waiting for the death that would release me from my torment and my senses were already beginning to blur, when suddenly, someone opened the door and entered it. I opened my eyes using my last strength and stared at the door, and I thought that I could see my cousin, Yukev Wilczynski. When Yukev looked at the moribund people, he got scared and immediately turned to run away. I called out to him with all my strength: "Yukev..." but my voice was weak. Yukev did not hear me and left. I understood that all was lost, that if there had been hope for a moment, it was gone.

But Yukev thought that he had heard someone call him. A few minutes later he retraced his steps. He looked at the moribund people and not recognising anyone, he decided to depart once again. Then I called him again with what was left of my strength: "Yukev..." I could not get a sound out or move a limb of my body. I opened my eyes and moved them, so that he would see that I was alive. He came nearer and when he finally recognised me, he almost fainted. I was in a horrible state, almost unrecognisable; I was at death's door. My beard and hair had grown wild, and I was skinny and dirty.

The elation was great, impossible to describe. First, he dragged me to the nearest forest together with a friend who was with him, so that if the Germans God forbid passed through the surroundings, they would not find us. They had a bit of food and water. To begin with he gave me some water with a spoon, one drop after another, and then he gave me something to eat. I recovered and ran away together with them.

I had been like a wanderer in the blazing desert who had run out of his water supply. I was exhausted, moribund, dying from thirst, when suddenly I awoke in the shade of palm trees, with a fountain of cool water in front of me. My cousin Yukev saved me from certain death and that was the first miracle that happened to me during the war.

In this manner Yukev and I wandered around burnt villages for a few days. There was nothing to eat, just some chickens that had survived here and there. Yukev was creative and resourceful and he took care of finding us food. He caught a chicken and slaughtered it with a piece of broken glass; we then cooked and ate it. Having grown up in a religious house, for me it was inconceivable to slaughter a chicken not according to Jewish law so that it would be kosher. In this respect, Yukev taught me how to survive.

At a certain point we left for the capital, Warsaw. We had heard that the battles against the Germans were still going on there and we joined the fighting. But the war had already been determined and we were taken prisoner, together with many other soldiers.

This was the beginning of a new era; "my period in captivity", and after it came "my period underground" and "my era of wanderings"; Here I will retell only a drop in the ocean of the struggles that I endured and lived through.

Captivity in Stalag A1

Yaakov: The Germans loaded us onto a freight train together with many other prisoners of war, squeezing us into the crowded carriages. We travelled like this day and night, without food or water, until we reached a snowy and cold area of Eastern Prussia. A prisoner of war camp called Stalag 1A was located there, near Bleichersdorf, in the Insterburg district of Konigsberg. It was situated within a forest on the Polish-German border.

When we reached our destination, the Germans separated the Polish captives from the Jewish ones. The Poles had plenty of food and drink, whereas we the Jews got almost nothing. Every morning we left to do forced-labour after receiving only small portions of bread and water.

We did hard physical labour; we built bridges and paved roads. Everything that the Germans had destroyed when they invaded Poland, we built anew. At night we slept in tents, on planks covered in straw. The conditions were harsh, the work was strenuous and food was scant. We suffered from hunger, cold, lice and disease, and we were always in fear of the Germans, who liked to beat us.

Every morning we found the corpses of dead people at the entrance to the tent; prisoners who had died of hunger; their heads lacking enough flesh and skin resembled skulls, their bodies, skin and bones. The Germans said that it was a pity to waste bullets on them, so they just let them die of hunger.

In order not to starve to death Yukev and I went to Klein Dexen. There we gathered rotting potatoes skins and bones left by the dogs from the Germans' garbage dump, and we ate them.

In the winter we heated the snow and melted it into water. In the summer, in order to avoid going mad with thirst, I would collect the waste waters that came out of the Germans' toilets and drank it; Yes! For lack of water I would drink the Germans' urine.

On Rosh Hashana I was in captivity in Stalag 1A in Eastern Prussia. At that time, I would have given a year of my life for a slice of bread and a glass of water to quench my thirst.

In order to keep some level of hygiene and fight off the lice, in the evenings we used to take tins, fill them with snow and boil our clothes in them. We did not have enough clothes to keep warm, so we suffered greatly from the cold. In order to keep our body temperatures normal, we used to cover ourselves with all sorts of strange things, for example, I used to put tins on the soles of my feet, and squeeze newspapers into them for warmth.

Below is a letter that I wrote to my sister Golda and my brother-in-law Haim Bierzwinski, who lived in Haifa during that time:

Bleichersdorf 10 December 1939
Dear sister and brother-in-law,

I would like to inform you that I survived the war in one piece and am healthy. I am currently located in a prisoner of war camp in Germany. However, I am worried - how are you my dear ones? How is your health? And how is dear Arel'ka? [Arela was the first- born daughter of Haim and Golda Bierzwinski]. I have written a few letters to our dear parents but have not received any reply, a thing that causes me great pain. This week, I received a postcard from my girlfriend [Pola Gliksman] from

Skulsk; even she did not mention how my parents are. I have no peace, not during the day and not at night.

Dearest sister, please reply as soon as possible if you can. How are you doing? How are things in Skulsk? And how are our Uncle, Aunt and Rachel doing? [Abraham and Regina Wilczynski.]

Yukev Wilczynski, the son of Bina from Sompolno, is also here with me. Today he received a postcard from Sompolno saying that all is well with them.

Please send me the address of dear Carla and Pola in Amsterdam, since I would like to ask them to send me some food items and I don't have their address.

Best Regards and warm-hearted
kisses to all of you. Your younger brother, Yaakov.

ps Please send heartfelt regards to my family and acquaintances.

Yaakov Eliezer Kotowski. 13.08.1939

My address: Prisoner of war, Kotowski Yaakov No.27318. Prisoner of War Camp, Stalag 1A, Postal Branch: Bleichersdorf, Insterburg District, Eastern Prussia, c/o Mrs. Plauman.

At a later stage, Yukev got work in the German's kitchen. Every day he would steal some food from there, bread or potatoes, and hide it in his clothes. In the evenings we used to sneak off and eat it. In spite of this we were always hungry and over time we became walking skeletons- skin and bones.

The prisoner of war camp was open, it was not surrounded by a fence since all around it were forests, and anyone who wanted to escape didn't have where to go.

The residents in the surroundings, who were Volksdeutsche, were loyal to the Germans and helped them. They were ordered not to help the prisoners of war, not to give them food, drink or anything else, and not to take them into their homes. The residents knew that whoever was caught helping the prisoners would have to bear the consequences, and the prisoners of war knew that anyone caught asking for anything, his blood be on his own head.

We were hungry, so one night we left for the villages that were in the surrounding area, further away from the camp, to ask for food. We reached one of the villages and in the yard of one of the houses we saw the landlord boiling water in a vat, inside which were rotten potatoes with their skins still on - food for his pigs. We were so hungry that we set upon the vat and started to grab potatoes from it, swallowing them while they were still extremely hot. The farmer who saw us was shocked and said to us: "Just a minute, wait a minute, leave these rotten potatoes, come into my house and I will give you something to eat."

I spoke German and Yukev did not. We agreed between us in advance that I should be the one to talk to the Germans, while he would pretend that he was mute, so that people would pity us even more, and so it was. The farmer brought us into his house, fed us and later gave each of us a parcel of food. Afterwards we approached a few more houses and received a few more parcels of food. When we had stocked up well, we headed back towards the camp.

Near the camp we dug some holes in the ground under a few trees, where we buried the food and covered it up with leaves, and each night we would return to open a parcel and eat from it.

On that night, the German commander of the camp unexpectedly decided to conduct a head count. He counted the prisoners of war and discovered that we were missing. When we returned, he called us to him and asked us where we had been. We told him that we had gone for a short walk in the nearby forest, and had gone to relieve ourselves. He roared at us, drew his pistol and gave us a good few blows to the face with it. Blood started to stream from my nose, he almost broke it. Later he held his pistol to my chest and said that if there were ever to be another head count and we were found missing, he would shoot us.

Yukev: One time in the middle of the night I heard people singing "Hatikva" [Israel's national anthem] and immediately afterwards shots were heard. I understood that there were Zionist Jews in the camp who had just been executed. Following this event, I understood what was in store for the Jews in the German prisoner of war camp, so I used a knife to cut a hatch in the Jewish camp tent I was in and ran from it to the Pole's prisoners of war tent. In retrospect, I think that this is what saved me.

Yaakov: We lived like this for nine months, until one day the order to release all the prisoners of war came. They gathered us for an assembly and announced that we were going to be released. We were very happy. The German foreman saw some smiling faces in the first tent, and then he called us and said: "Dear brothers, up until now you have been living in paradise, soon you will enter the gates of hell and then you will wish for death." Then we thought to ourselves: Can anything be worse than what we went through in the camp?

Regrettably he was right, we could not imagine into what a terrible reality we were about to enter.

They gave every prisoner of war a package of food: Bread, jam and some water. They put us on a train that went from Insterburg in Eastern Prussia, to Lublin in Poland. It was a cargo train for animals. All the way from Prussia to Lublin they did not open the train even once. It was unbearably crowded. By the time we reached Lublin people on the train had died from hunger, thirst, disease, fatigue, lice and mere exhaustion. From there, whoever was still alive, we scattered one by one to our respective homes.

Yukev and I walked together all the way from Lublin on foot. It was a long walk, about four hundred kilometres. Luckily, people gave us food and drink in every place we passed. We reached Yukev's family in Sompolno first and then I continued to Skulsk.

When I reached Skulsk I was afraid to just go into our house. I was worried that my parents would get a terrible shock, I was in a deteriorated state, with long hair and a beard and I was very undernourished. They had not seen me for almost a year and had not heard anything from me; they thought that I had been killed. To ease the shock, I went to our neighbours' house first, the house of Aunt Salka, who was my father's sister and the mother of my cousin Moishe Biderko. From there I sent my aunt to my parents' house to tell them that I had returned, and that I was at their house.

It is impossible to describe the excitement; my parents came running, my mother in tears. They took me home and all the family was united once again. There was great joy at home. My married sisters Pola and Carla were in Holland, Golda was in Israel and at home there were six of us: Mother, father, Hanna, Ida, Yehudah and myself.

When I returned, the Germans had already started to persecute the Jews; what the future held for us we did not know.

The "Shtetl"

Hanna: By 1933 rumours had started to reach us about the iniquities of Hitler, the great Nazi enemy in Germany. We heard reports over the radio, in addition to which the first people who were deported from Germany reached Poland and told us what was happening first hand.

Aharon Leib's flat had been left orphaned; therefore, it was let out to a teacher and his family who were Volksdeutsche. We kept our distance from them, since we suspected that he was a German spy; and indeed, this assumption proved to be right, because when the Germans invaded Poland the Volksdeutsche helped them beyond all expectation, to adjust, acclimatize and operate in their new surroundings.

With the outbreak of war on 1st September 1939, the Germans conquered our town within the first hours, since it was located not far from the German border. Within a few days all of Poland had been conquered by the Germans. The town was shocked, as was the whole of Poland. The first refugees who reached us were residents of the Poznan region. They had escaped inland, to the east, out of fear of the Germans. They had left their houses because the German soldiers were looting and killing as much as they possibly could, for no apparent reason and without justification. Cattle and people from all directions intertwined with each other out of panic and fear. The

Polish army raised barbed wire fences in order to stop the Germans' advance, but in retrospect it turned out that this was ineffective. There was no choice but to wait and see what each day would bring. Life became more unbearable from day to day.

Everybody was trying to escape and people scattered throughout the land, an anarchic situation was created and there was no authority or government. Jews from all over the surrounding towns, of Poznan, Inowroclaw, Strzelno, Kruszwica and Bydgoszcz, ran away not knowing where they were headed, they were now refugees escaping from the killings that were taking place in their hometowns.

Sometime after the German invasion of Poland mother returned from her visit to Holland. Yaakov was drafted into the army once again and there were just five of us left at home: Father, mother, Ida, Yehudah and me.

Clashes started between the Poles and the Volksdeutsche and the Poles started lynching Germans.

At the end of September 1939, in spite of battles that were still going on in Warsaw, which had not yet been conquered, the Germans entered our town. At that point, the Volksdeutsche, with the support of the invaders, dared demonstrate their bravery and started to take revenge on the Poles for the killing of their German brothers.

One day, thirty Poles who had killed Germans were caught; they were mainly youths off the streets. They tried to put the blame on the Jews and claimed that my brother (Yehudah) had taken part in the killings. The Gestapo [the secret Nazi state police] of Konin, the county's main city, came to take them. Chained and handcuffed they were led away without trial to the jail in Konin, where two months later they were executed. Luckily, some other Germans from the adjacent villages who had contacts with Father spoke out and requested my brother be set free, since they knew that he was not guilty, and so he was saved.

The first Jewish site that fell victim to the raids in our town was the synagogue. On Rosh Hashana the Germans attacked it armed with axes and hatchets, smashing and destroying everything that they could, even the stoves and walls were not spared from destruction. Out of fright and shock we all ran away from the calamity that fell on us to the nearby villages. We were afraid of what the future would bring; fortunately, there were no casualties at that point.

The Germans slowly started to get familiar with the area. All the office positions were taken by the Volksdeutsche and we, the younger generation, were forced to go out and work. We did various hard and despised jobs, the dirtiest work. The women worked in the houses of the German women, and cleaned offices. The men dealt with disposing of bombs that the Germans had dropped, dismantling barbed wire and clearing mines that the Poles had concealed. Every day they left in groups of thirty; sometimes mines exploded and then the Poles would laugh: "It's nothing, never mind, just a few more dead Jews." Luckily, there were no casualties.

Various assets were taken away and transferred to the hands of the trusted allies of the Germans; they in turn rejoiced and were delighted at the expense of the Jews. A trusted ally such as this could walk into a Jewish shop and take anything that he liked for himself, while the Jewish shop owner was then ordered to carry out the goods himself to their carriage. And if that wasn't enough, they were never satisfied until they also abused the poor guy; Jews were ordered to fall to the ground, stand up, run back and forth, whippings were dished out, and so forth.

The Poles also had a chance to demonstrate their hate of the Jews; suckled from the milk of their mothers' they despised "Israel" (the Jewish People) from birth. They did not miss any opportunity to destroy us completely; they beat us and humiliated us in any place and on every occasion.

I had a blue and white painted kayak, with the name "Tel Aviv" written on it, and I used to sail it on the lake in the summertime. A

Polish friend of mine called Tadeusz Kloczowski, who was supposed to stand up for me came with the Germans and took it from me. I cried and called out to him: "How could you do such a thing to me? We are good friends ", and he replied: "Get lost, shitty Jewess, I don't know you".

At the time I had a boyfriend from the town called Zigmunt Nasielski, we had planned to get married. There was a Polish girl who loved him too and also wanted to marry him. When she heard that Zigmunt was intending to marry me she came to me and said: "If you marry Zigmunt I shall inform on you and all your family to the Germans." I, who knew what the meaning of what she had said to me was, said nothing. She took Zigmunt to the church and there she married him. She probably convinced him that in this way he would be saved, and indeed he was saved.

The rich farmers from the Poznan area were uprooted and deported from their lands. The Volksdeutsche took care of this matter willingly and imaginatively; in such cases they did whatever they wished. If the German was a good person, he would allow the farmers to take some things with them, others would send the farmers away like dogs, with nothing.

Life became more impossible from day to day and there was despair everywhere. Trade was already forbidden for the Jews; therefore, we would all earn whatever we could on the black market. A small consolation was the fact that the police in our town were not German, but Austrian. They did not participate in dire deeds such us killing people, as was the case in the neighbouring towns. Thus, things continued until July 1940.

We noticed that the Germans were preparing themselves for something - we didn't know what. A few days before the uprooting of our family from our home, while speculation and fear gnawed at our hearts, mother was collecting flower seeds, as was her custom every year, for sowing in the garden the following year. The teacher who was our tenant passed by and said to her: "Mrs. Kotowski, you are collecting the seeds but others will sow them. "She did not understand what he meant, but he probably already knew about the plans to deport the Jews.

Yaakov: I returned home from captivity and all hell broke out, just as promised. When Hitler's soldiers entered our town the first thing they did, was to kill the dogs since they were afraid of them. They killed Zefirka with one bullet; on the other hand, they did not succeed in killing Rozboj so easily. I counted eight bullets shot at him before his heart stopped and they managed to kill him. This was one of the most difficult things that I experienced, I cried and Hanna cried too.

The Deportations

The First Deportation

The first deportation was to the Konin region. They gathered all the Jews from Skulsk and from the adjacent towns and we were deported to a neighbouring town in the surrounding area. They didn't let us take much from our homes. Labour camps were erected where we were taken, and everybody was forced to do hard labour, for example clearing stones and rocks and paving roads that had been destroyed during the German bombardments. We organised ourselves, two families in one house; we worked together and ate together. The situation was difficult but still bearable.

Hanna: On the 12th of July 1940, towards evening, some tension was felt in the town, as if a storm was about to break, people felt as if something was going to happen that night. We saw carriages and carts that had been ordered to stand at street corners. Since it was forbidden to go out onto the street after seven in the evenings, once in a while someone would sneak out of their house quietly and go to the neighbours, to try and glean some information, if there was any, about what was about to happen. The whole thing was organised in a sophisticated manner, nobody knew anything and no one could have guessed what was about to happen. No one could sleep, we all sat and waited anxiously for what was about to take place. Who was destined for deportation first, the Polish farmers or us the Jews?

Then something happened; at 2 o'clock in the morning screams could be heard. In the beginning we didn't know where they were coming from. We were trembling with fear, when suddenly there were strong knocks at our door; the "Gendarmerie" and two Volksdeutsche were shouting at us: "You have ten minutes to get dressed, take twenty kilograms per person, not one gram more, and leave the house."

The deportation of the Jews had started. The Jews gathered near the Committee's Community building. Our minds filled with trepidation; where would they deport us to? What would they do with us? Nobody knew. Nobody had the answer. In some houses people were beaten, people cried and pleaded to be left alone, but nothing helped.

Mother insisted she didn't want to leave, and said: "if you send me away from my home, from the house I live in, it will kill me." The soldier who took us immediately said to her: "You will not have long to wait; others will do the job…" Afterwards, when mother wanted to wear a nicer dress, the policeman told her decisively that her dress was too nice and ordered her to go and change immediately.

The Gendarmerie and the Volksdeutsche started looting straight away. They each filled their pockets with whatever they could get their hands on, from all the best that we had in the house. We stood on our feet waiting till the morning hours, when the carts started to come. On 13th July 1940 they loaded us onto about thirty carts that stood in a convoy one after the other. Accompanied by the Gendarmerie, we passed the towns and villages where we were born, where we grew up, where we were educated and to which we were connected, and left behind everything that we had ever known. We travelled not knowing where we were going to. On the roads we saw all the horrors that the Germans had carried out and we knew that not all of us would return.

We passed the adjacent town of Slesin on the way and witnessed the same tragedy there. All the Jews had been deported at night by carts; there too, the Poles stood by with joyful faces, watching the deportation of the Jews from street corners, as we went onwards to Konin. In Konin there weren't many Jewish families left, since some of them had already been deported to Ostrowiec Mazowiezki in Christmas of 1939; those who were left were joined with us for deportation. All in all we were taken from five towns.

After a seven hour journey we reached the town of Grodziec in the Konin district. There in the market we saw Jews from the nearby towns; there were cries and wailing, people who did not know what to do, they had been thrown into the street with their children and infants, and with what little possessions they had managed to take.

Towards evening the Gendarmerie tried to cram us in, somewhere between all the Jewish and Christian families, pushing us into every corner and every possible space; but the town was small and there wasn't enough room for everybody, so again we were loaded onto the carts and were sent to the next nearby village called Krolikow, about five kilometres from Grodziec; and here a new tragedy began. Where would we start? How would we live?

Since Grodziec belonged to the Konin district, the "Krajschef", the police commander and the rest of the policemen of the Gendarmerie, were all well-known to everybody. Jews received pass certificates and could travel secretly to Skulsk, Slesin or Konin, to look for and take whatever they had managed to hide. People snuck into their own homes at night, but woe betide anyone who was caught. They would return following murderous beatings.

There was one Jew from Konin; his name was Artur Lipszyc, who tried to reach his house in this way. As fate would have it he was caught by the Gestapo and shot on the spot, his body was sent to his mother.

We started to get used to this life. We lived in wooden sheds and were forced to do hard labour, work that is difficult to describe. A working day lasted for ten hours. We cleaned offices; we cleaned streets and cleared snow. Again, the women worked at the houses of the German wives and the men dealt with the disposing of bombs and clearing of mines.

In the winter, about sixty men and three women were sent back to a town called Kleczew. The men were forced to work in the cemeteries, to clear the ground of the remains of skulls and bones, which they were later ordered to throw into the water. The Gestapo and "Volksdeutsche" who supervised them didn't stop abusing and beating them.

One night, the German police burst in, threw out the men and attacked the girls. The girls aged sixteen and seventeen burst out in screams, shots were fired and they prevented the men from going back in. The girls, scratched, bleeding and with torn clothes managed to escape and ran screaming in the streets. This event reached the ears of the commander of the police station, the "Krajschef", who took the matter into his own hands. He passed the information on to Poznan and they then liquidated the camp in Kleczew, and the German policemen were sent to the front.

So, it was for seven months, all the while we waited to see what our destiny would be. The situation was unstable and all the time there were rumours that we would be sent off to another place. Once again, the quiet before the storm came, a feeling that could be sensed in every corner, and people started to huddle together out of fear.

The Second Deportation

The second deportation took place on 15th February 1941. A decree was issued by the Gendarmerie to pack our belongings. Where to this time? Not a word, it was a secret. At four o'clock in the afternoon a cart stood in front of each house where Jews resided and everyone loaded as much as they could of their most important and needed belongings.

Yaakov: We were left almost without any possessions and without any money. We knew that we had to safeguard the little money that we still had. It was a well-known fact to everyone that the Poles, Ukrainians and Germans would search every corner, including body searches. We decided to swallow some bank notes; we had notes of 500 zloty. We rolled the notes up tightly and spread castor oil on them, so that they would be easier to swallow. One after the next we each tried to swallow a note, but everyone threw up the notes, only I succeeded. I swallowed three notes of 500 zloty each.

Hanna: It was already dark outside when we left, again accompanied by the Gendarmerie and the "Volksdeutsche". We travelled about three kilometres in a convoy, one cart after another, towards Konin. Suddenly shouts and cries were heard, there was a commotion. The Gestapo turned up ahead of us and we were transferred into their hands, we were no longer under the control of the police. On the way we suffered hits and blows from whips and clubs, and in this manner, we reached the railway station in Konin. They pushed us into a train carriage by kicking and beating us. Before they had managed to push us all into the carriage, behold a new order came, accompanied by screams and whippings, and we were ordered to get out and move to another train. Mothers lost their children, children lost their parents, and all hell broke loose. We were ordered to throw all our belongings, the things that we had brought with us, into a heap; we were not allowed to bring anything onto the train. Our torments continued the entire night.

Towards morning the men were ordered to leave the carriages and to go to the station's square. Shouts and cries were heard again as nobody knew what the reason for this was. They were ordered to put all our belongings onto a separate carriage and afterwards they were instructed to gather all the rubbish and sand that was scattered on the station's floor and put it into the same carriage. Since there were no brooms, they swept the floor with their hats. "We don't want you and your rubbish. We don't want to see you anymore," screamed the Gestapo men, all the while beating and whipping us. And then the train departed and went on its way. We were lucky that the train left.

The following morning, they unloaded us at the Lodz ghetto, and put us all in an empty factory building. Another night of fear passed. What would happen to us? What would they do with us? And then we were abused again; we underwent a humiliating and painful physical search, the aim of which was to take anything that they could from us. The search was meticulous; they looked in every possible place, even in our body cavities. Those who conducted the search were both Gestapo, but also just ordinary people off the streets; they were all drunk and had truncheons in their hands. The sound of loud music being played over speakers could be heard, in order to mute the screams of the people that were being abused. Older people fell down and fainted, nobody paid any attention to them. Simultaneously, the young people were taken to work; they gathered sixty men and eight women to work in the "Reichsbahn Dienst" [The German Railways Office].

All this lasted for two days and two nights, during that time we didn't get any food or water. Finally, they made us stand in groups of four and under the guard of the Gestapo, made us run for three or four hours through the streets of Lodz, to the railway station, where we were once again loaded onto the train carriages, which were sealed so that nobody could escape.

The train travelled for eight days and eight nights and we were inside the closed and sealed carriages without any food or water. The winter weather was cruel to us too; It was freezing, a cold that cannot be described. People fell, fainted, and collapsed from weakness, hunger and thirst. There were no toilets. People died of starvation and dehydration. Many children perished, their souls leaving them on the way in front of the agonizing eyes of their parents who could do nothing to save them. The corpses were left lying on the carriage's floor; others were pushed into corners, the stench was terrible, it was impossible to sit down. When the train stopped at a station for a few moments on the way, and another train from the opposite direction also stopped, the engine driver would hand us a cooking pot containing mouldy water. Each of us took a sip using a spoon so that whoever was next would also be able to wet their dry and cracked lips that had burst from thirst and dryness. On one occasion, when the train stopped at a station and the Gendarmes could not see him, my father asked the engine driver to give us some water, and he did. Again, people received a bit of water, tiny drops, even if only to wet their lips. Under these conditions, children were born and the elderly passed away, the despair was great.

We continued to travel further, towards Lublin. On the way we saw the ghetto of Kutno, which was later burnt down, together with all its inhabitants. We stopped in a few places, and at every stop we were told: "You are getting off here", but after a couple of hours we continued and travelled further. From the "Warthegau" [The part of Western Poland that was incorporated into the Reich and "Germanized" by the persecution and deportation of undesirables], we were forced to leave to the "Generalgouvernement" [an administrative unit established by the Germans, consisting of those parts of Poland that were not incorporated into the Reich]. Everywhere was over-populated and bursting at the seams with people, therefore no community wanted to receive us, even the Gestapo didn't know what to do with us.

Holland

Jopie: I had a nice childhood in Holland. At school I studied together with gentile children, up until the German invasion of Holland.

In Amsterdam we lived near the "Artis" zoo, at 7a Plantage Franselaan street, which today is called Polaklaan street. On our street the chief Rabbi of Amsterdam, Sar-Louis, also lived.

When the war broke out in Europe in 1939, I was eight years old. Father had told me about the war that was taking place in Europe, but as children in Amsterdam we continued to study together with the gentile children, up until the Germans occupied Holland. The Germans aggrieved the Jews in a very sophisticated way. They did everything in stages.

On 10th January 1940 the Germans invaded Holland and conquered it. They started to gradually expropriate Jewish businesses. It was forbidden to wander around in the streets after seven o'clock in the evening and starting from 1942 Jews were given the order to wear the yellow star.

In 1941 the Germans started to take control of Jewish businesses. Factories were confiscated; all the owners of assets were banished from their work-place and in their place Dutch managers, who were collaborating with the German authorities, were instated. Our business was taken over by a Dutchman called Gillet who was himself a producer of confectionary.

At that time, my grandfather, Menachem Mendel Landau, passed away and a special certificate of approval for the funeral was required to bury him outside Amsterdam since Jews were not allowed to leave the city. The certificate was obtained and the funeral took place outside the city. I didn't go to the funeral.

After the German invasion of Amsterdam in 1941, father became ill with angina pectoris and was admitted to the temporary Jewish hospital N.I.Z, which was located in the French Boulevard.

After father recovered from his illness he returned home. He used to go for a walk in the streets close to our house every day; one day he met Avraham Sar-Louis, who was the son of the Chief Rabbi of Amsterdam. The same Sar-Louis met father at a later stage in Westerbork and was witness to the transport in which my family was taken from Holland. Before he parted from father, father made him swear that if he survived, he would help me reach Palestine.

Avraham Sar-Louis also fell sick during the time of the war, he had tuberculosis, and so that he would not infect other people he was put in isolation; by some miracle he survived and I shall elaborate more about him later.

In the year 1942 all the Jewish children were expelled from the mixed schools where the gentiles studied. The Jewish children started to learn in their own study groups and then the order for the Jews to wear the yellow star was also decreed.

At that time the noose was being tightened around the neck of the Jews. A curfew was declared and the Jews were ordered to prepare to be taken away to work camps.

Father and my uncle Pinhas began to worry about what to do with us, the children.

Roza, Pinhas' youngest daughter, was transferred through the Dutch underground to a Christian family in the north of Holland, where she served as a house maid.

Lyia was given to our Dutch neighbours, Pieter and Anna Beun.

One of the other neighbours informed on her and the Germans came to look for her. Our neighbours hid her behind a heavy curtain that they had in their house. The Germans looked for her but didn't find her and this is how she was saved.

In the apartment building where we lived there were four flats; my family's, my uncle Pinhas' and two flats that belonged to some Dutch people. Each family had store-rooms in which to keep their belongings or stock coal. There was a gap between the store- rooms and it was through this gap that father passed to the Dutch neighbours' apartments in order to get updates about the situation, on their radio.

In June 2012, an ad that had been published in a Jewish newspaper on the 14th of January 1943 was discovered online; in it, my mother Pola announced that father had reached the age of fifty and that she hoped that we could celebrate his birthday.

Eventually the "Aktzias" [round up of Jews] began. The Germans started to fill vehicles with people; first with those who volunteered to go freely, and then if they did not manage to fill the vehicles, they would start "hunting" people down in order to fill the quota.

When my parents understood that we had reached the stage when the Germans would be coming to take entire families out of their homes to go to the work camps, it was decided to hide me and my sister Shulamit, who was then five years old, above the top store-room.

Shulamit and I were in the attic when an Allied attack suddenly started. Alarms went off, there were explosions and a horrible noise, Shulamit was scared and she cried. My parents decided to bring her down from the attic so that I would not be discovered. So I lay down in the attic, a child of ten or eleven, and I heard how the Germans came to take away all the neighbours living in flats 1, 2, 3 and 4.

I lay there frozen and scared. I had some food. Suddenly I heard somebody's footsteps coming up the stairs and I saw two Germans through the cracks of the floor, talking to each other and saying: "Where is the child?" I was the one who could see but could not be seen. They looked for me all over the house and fortunately they didn't find me. In the end they went back down and closed up the house.

In retrospect I found out two things: first, that after the Germans had left they had closed the house with a seal, and second that a Dutch neighbour who had seen who had come out of the house informed the Germans that there was still a boy in our house (me), and an additional girl on the lower ground floor (Lyia, who was hidden at the neighbour's flat). As I previously said,
they looked for us but luckily didn't find us.

All the Jews who had been taken out of their homes were concentrated at a location three streets away from our home, where they were all assembled in the theatre building. They gathered all the children and took them to the other side of the road. There were attempts to smuggle Shulamit out, but with no success. They stayed there for two weeks, after which a transport that passed through the railway station of Westerbork was organized. There was additional transport to Sobibor from Westerbork, and Sobibor is where they were murdered.

Westerbork was a transit camp in Holland. It had originally been established by the Dutch government for refugees from Germany who had escaped to Holland illegally. After the occupation, the Germans turned it into a transit camp for "Transports to the East", to the death camps of Auschwitz and Sobibor.

Sobibor was an extermination camp in the district of Lublin, in Poland. On May 8th 1942 the murderous acts began. The sole objective of the camp was extermination. About 260,000 Jews, of which 32,000 were from Holland, perished here. On Liberation Day, only nineteen survivors were found in Sobibor.

Uncle Pinhas was a member of the Dutch underground and had the opportunity to escape from this fate, but when father, mother and Shulamit were taken to Westerbork, he was not prepared to be separated from them, and consequently determined his destiny and also that of his wife Sara. They were all sent to Sobibor, never to return. At a later stage, someone who escaped from the death train told me that he was in the same carriage as my father and according to him father had already died on the train, before he reached the extermination camp. In 1946 after the war, while I was still in Holland, I received a letter from the Red Cross which stated that Avraham, Pola and Shulamit Landau were transferred from Westerbork to Sobibor and perished there.

Our Dutch neighbour, Anna Beun had promised my parents that if I survive, she would take care of me in exchange for money, and so it was. After a few days, once the Aktzias in the area had finished, she sent her son Anton for me.

In the meantime, I had been in the attic for four to six days. Then Anton, the neighbour's son, came and told me to come down, to take off my yellow star, and to get out of the house and go in the direction of the basketball court that was close to our house. There, so he told me, a man riding a bicycle, whose description I had previously been given, would be waiting for me. This man would take me to where necessary. It turned out that the man was a member of the Dutch underground. This organization helped a lot of Jews. Anton also told me that Lyia my cousin was at their house.

I did what I was told to do. We went to another quarter of Amsterdam by bicycle, and I stayed there for at least two weeks. During this time a temporary solution was found for me. I was transferred to a farm owned by the Van Zanten family. They also belonged to the Dutch underground and they were asked to look after me. They organised a certificate from the Red Cross for me and I was given a new name, that of a Dutch boy who had been killed in the bombing of Rotterdam, Jan Vermeulen.

I stayed in this village for about two or three weeks, after which it was decided to move me again because it became known that there was a collaborator in the local police. I was immediately smuggled to the Gelderland district in the east of Holland and taken to a small village called Nederhemert, where there was a woman living on her own with her only son; her husband worked far from home. In that village there was a castle belonging to the Count Van Wassenaar, who was a member of one of the Dutch nobility dynasties. He was renowned as a supporter of the ideology of the Nazi occupier in Holland. I stayed in this village for four to five months, during which I even befriended the son of the Count. Afterwards somebody informed on me and again I was smuggled to yet another district.

I reached the district of Limburg, the southern most district of Holland, a German district, arriving at a village to a village called Grubbenvorst, where I was handed over to the Verbeek family.

Mrs Anna Beun was the one who took me from place to place, and she also brought me here by train.

The Verbeek family had a few children; an eldest daughter, whose name I cannot recall and three other children: Pierre, Joep and Jan. Seeing as I was the youngest, they nicknamed me "little Jan."

The parents of the Verbeek family with whom I stayed knew that I was a Jew of course, but their children did not. They had a grocery shop and a maize farm; I spent the rest of my time until the end of the war with them.

In this village there was a good-hearted priest, Pater Henri Vullings, who decided to help many Jews and he made sure that families from the village would hide them. In retrospect I found out that he had organised the entire underground movement in the village where I had stayed. There were many hills in the area in which a poultry enclosure had been constructed, behind this there was a door which led to a large hiding place. Many Jews were hidden there and the priest took care of them. In the end the priest was caught, badly tortured and sent to the extermination camp Bergen Belzen where he perished. At a later stage a square was built in the village and a statue erected, to commemorate his name.

Carla: On 10th May 1940 the Germans conquered Holland. In the beginning we didn't feel their presence. The Germans behaved in a different manner towards the Dutch Jews than they did towards the Jews of Poland, but they were preparing everything meticulously, in co-operation with the "Judenrats" [Jewish Councils], through which they obtained the names and addresses of all the Jews in Holland.

The Judenrats were Jewish controlled institutions that were appointed to mediate between the Nazi authorities and the Jewish communities. They were temporary institutions that were destined, in retrospect, to fulfil the German policy that preceded the "Final Solution" of "The Jewish Question". Judenrats were established by order of the Germans, in all the Jewish communities of the conquered territories in Europe during the holocaust.

We could feel the consequences of the decrees that were being passed in relation to us from the start. To begin with, they started to gradually expropriate the businesses of the Jews. In our case they occupied the factory only in 1942, until then we worked in the factory without any disturbances. At a certain point a Dutch man came to the factory together with a German man, and the management of the business was passed into his hands. He told my husband that he could stay in the business, but his partner was told to go home immediately. Gradually they started to bring in new workers and one day, the Dutch man who had taken over the management, told my husband to go home and not to return.

When the Germans started to expropriate the businesses of the Jews, they had to deal with the protests of the Dutch people, because they foresaw that this would mean trouble for the Dutch people too. I have to say that the Christians did a lot at the time, they protested profusely.

During this period there were difficulties, unpleasant things were happening, but it was nothing like the persecution of the Jews in Poland. We felt that something was about to happen but we had no idea what it would be. We refused to believe that in Holland something could happen to the Jews. The Dutch didn't support the German's persecution of the Jews; they were different from the Poles. We felt that a storm was brewing, things weren't peaceful for us, but we couldn't imagine that we would be forced to leave everything we ever had. The general feeling was that nothing as bad as physical extermination was in store for the Jewry of Holland. This was a bitter mistake; in the early days we just couldn't imagine where the German occupation would lead.

In the beginning we got letters from our parents in Poland, regularly. We sent them food packages and even money. Everything reached them within a reasonable time. This was true up until 1942, until the very last day before we were expelled from Holland.

At some point, they started to put limitations on our movements. After 7 o'clock in the evening it was forbidden to be on the streets. The Jews were forced to wear the yellow star in 1942. We only had three months to wear the star. In addition, the Germans demanded we hand over our gold, radios and other possessions.

On the same day my husband was sent home from work we received a letter in which we were asked to present ourselves for the first "transport", which was to be on the 14th of July 1942. My husband said that we would not go to the transport. We had some good Christian friends who had offered us a place to hide. But at that time, hiding in other people's homes was not yet customary among the Jews. My husband was a very proud and very optimistic man, and since he did not think that anything bad would happen to us, he said that we should not go into hiding.

One day, we were out on the streets of Amsterdam, when we met an acquaintance who told us that on that night there would be a bus available on which we could escape. There were already fourteen places taken on the bus and two places left to fill the vehicle. The driver had been persuaded, for a considerable sum of money, to take all the passengers to Switzerland. If we wanted to join, we had to bring a certain sum of money and come...

We returned home and took the most essential things that were in our possession with us. We were unable to part from David's parents since it was already late and we planned to join the bus.

On that night the first transport got on its way. They needed to gather 1400 or 1500 people for the transport. To begin with letters were sent out to those who were on the list for that transport. Since most people didn't present themselves freely for the expulsion, they decided to make up the numbers by an initiated "hunt". The Gestapo caught people in the streets and also dragged people from their homes and took them by force to the transport. While they were out looking for people for the transport, we snuck out towards the group that had prepared to escape, and when we got there, we met people that we knew. Each person had taken their most precious possessions with them. So many precious things, such treasures were collected there on that night that it is beyond description. The people in question were very rich. And so, we gathered on that night, sixteen of us, and boarded the bus, all horribly frightened.

From the outside the vehicle looked as if it was transporting iron. After ten minutes the bus started moving and was immediately stopped at the first check point in Amsterdam. The driver said that he was transporting iron and presented the delivery note. They let us pass and we went on. After an additional ten minutes we were stopped again and documents were requested once more. "Are you only transporting iron?" they asked and instructed the driver to park on the side of the road. Suddenly, they burst into the bus, removed its fake walls, and of course discovered all of us. When we saw the Germans, we could see death staring us in the face. They had caught sixteen "criminals" and they led us straight to the Gestapo.

They beat us badly, instructed us to squat on our knees and put each of us in a separate room in order to search us and take whatever we had on us. In retrospect we understood that the driver who had taken us for money was probably a Dutch fascist.

At that time, it was forbidden for Jews to hold gold, silver or any other items of value. Each of us gave over any items of value we had in our possession. I was fourth in line. I glanced over at the table, where all the seized items were gathered, and I thought about the financial gain that the Germans would have from our possessions. Some of my jewellery was sewn inside my clothes and I didn't give it to them; even though it was a risk, I was ready to bear the consequences. I only put what was in my pockets on the table.

They hurt us badly, they beat us relentlessly, and afterwards each of us was transferred to a different prison in Amsterdam. I didn't know where my husband was and he didn't know where I was.

That was how we spent the night. The following day we started witnessing heart-breaking scenes. We saw hundreds of children who had been rounded up crying. We met a lot of our acquaintances. We were held separately. That night they led us to the main railway station; they put us onto train carriages and transferred us to Westerbork, there I met my husband again. It is difficult to describe my happiness when we were reunited.

In Westerbork the Germans had built a camp in which they concentrated the Jews that were caught, and from there they were sent to different destinations. Westerbork was a transit camp and from it transports were made to the death camps.

Carla and David Lewenhoff Amsterdam 14.01.1939

Jozefow Bilgorajski

Hanna: We reached Jozefow on 22nd February 1941. Jozefow, which was a smaller town than Skulsk, had been largely destroyed and burnt down. The houses had no doors or windows because at the beginning of September 1939 the town had been bombarded by German planes which had passed through on their way to the Russian border. Consequently, most of the town's houses had gone up in flames and very few inhabitable houses were left. The soil was sandy in the area and there was a quarry, the town itself was surrounded by forests.

We could hardly stand on our feet when we were thrown like rags into a railway station that was about 3 km away from the town called Jozefow, in the district of Bilgoraj. The town was located about ninety kilometres from the city of Lublin and not far from the Russian border. The mayor of the town awaited us there accompanied by a dog that randomly started to bite people, exhausted and starved as we were. In much the same way as the other officials that we had encountered on the way "the poor man" didn't know what to do with us. The Gestapo also had big vicious dogs with them, who were much like themselves, and which indiscriminately bit us, as they stood by and laughed with unconcealed pleasure.

After that, the Gestapo left and we could see that we were no longer under their supervision. We felt freer but we didn't know where to go or what to do. We asked the Poles where we were and if there were any

Jews around. Some of the young men who felt strong enough scattered around the area, and consequently the Jews of Jozefow learnt of us and of our predicament. The town's Rabbi [Szymon Parzeczewski] came to us, accompanied by the people of the Jewish community and they tried to help. Carts were brought and the sick among us were taken to the town. They were a handful of good people who received us with open arms and much warmth, while they themselves were poor and subjugated to the Ukrainians and the Poles. In spite of this they did their best so that each and every one of us would have a place to rest our frozen bodies and recover.

Later another real and almost unsolvable situation arose; where were we to put an additional 1300 people, in this small place that was already densely populated? Families started to organise themselves in groups of five or six wherever possible. They settled in corridors or any possible space that they could find. A committee was established to take care of all the ensuing problems. We were living ten people to a room. The circumstances were difficult and I can't describe the living conditions. Our lives were worse than the lives of dogs and cats on the street. Paucity and hunger were the norm for everyone.

In Jozefow we were under Polish rule, the Head of the Community and the Commander of the Police were Poles and above them were the Germans. The Germans, the Poles and the Ukrainians saw themselves as our keepers; they could all do whatever they wanted with us.

After a few days of rest, the Judenrat was organised and an order was given that all the young people had to register and would have to go to work. [During a certain period, Ida also worked at the Judenrat. This was in the period before the outbreak of war between Germany and Russia, which was called "Operation Barbarossa"]. The roads all around us were dirt tracks; therefore the Jews were forced to pave roads. We went to work every day from six o'clock in the morning till five o'clock in the afternoon, just before sunset. In snow, rain and wind; nothing would prevent the continuation of work. It was necessary to pave the roads at any cost, all under the watchful eyes of the "Wehrmacht" [The unified armed forces of Nazi Germany]. The women were forced to carry rocks, to erect supports and to dig trenches, the men chiselled the rocks. The paving of the roads was done by the German soldiers themselves.

We would return home at the end of each working day hungry, soaking wet and sad. There was nowhere we could even dry our wet clothes. The wages were so meagre that it was barely sufficient to buy about a kilogram of brown bread.

There were also other places of work in the surroundings, for example at a Polish estate owner's called Arendowski, who had ordered Jews for work. He took the men to cut wood in the forests and the girls worked planting trees; but he took advantage of the situation and any young woman he didn't like was transferred into the hands of the police, where she was punished by beatings, ten days of arrest and a monetary fine. There was also work at the sawmill of the Gorecki brothers. They too knew how to take full advantage of the situation. The workers were supplied by the Jewish Committee, which was under the supervision of the Polish community.

We were treated badly. The police were made up of Germans, Poles and Ukrainians, and all of them could do whatever they wanted to us with no constraints. Every day all of us had to report to the Polish Committee. The head of the Polish community always held a truncheon in his hand, with which he would beat and kick anybody his heart desired. Afterwards they would transfer us to our place of work. Not everyone got the privilege of eating something on a daily basis, since not everyone had where to get food, nobody asked us about this. We tried to stay in good spirits, as much as this was possible, and everyone worked far beyond what little energy they still had in order to stay alive.

Rumours started to reach us about what had happened to the Jews in the Warthegau. Polish acquaintances wrote to us that the Jews of the town of Zagorowa were sent to an unknown location. This happened on the 6th of February 1941, they just disappeared off the face of the earth, and until this very day no one knows what their fate was or how they were killed.

The German army started their movement towards Russia during this period, battalion after battalion passed through during the day, and during the night fires were seen in all directions, accompanied by the melody of firearms. And fear grew even greater in the hearts of the Jews. What would happen now? People started to pack their belongings, to dig shelters and ditches, there was tumult, and we were forbidden to go out onto the streets after six in the evening. We crowded together in small rooms; it was summer and the heat made things worse, exhausted children, lacking air to breathe, food and water, became swollen and dehydrated.

Operation Barbarossa was launched on 22nd June 1941. 3.9 million soldiers, most of them Germans, launched a surprise attack on the Soviet Union. The front moved farther and farther away into the depths of Russia. In our area there was no resistance at all and this fact was in our favour. We had a few months of peace; we went to work every day and waited to see what would happen.

Rosh Hashana in Jozefow took place on 22nd September 1941 and brought with it a bit of festivity. Two places for prayer were organised with the approval of the police. One location was in the flat of the Rabbi, the other was in the destroyed synagogue. They tried to set up these locations for the occasion, found benches for the congregation, and everyone tried to dress as best they could in order to look festive.

The first day passed quietly. The Rabbi prayed in his flat and in the synagogue, the prayer was led by Mendele the Shoychet. He was a young man, about 35 years of age, who was quiet and calm, devoted to prayer and to God alone. In days of normalcy he had done public work and had collected donations to help others. Word had it, that at the beginning of the war he was accused and arrested for kosher slaughtering in secret. However, as was customary in our community, a bribe had been given, he was redeemed and the matter was overlooked. After a year the matter was completely forgotten...

After the festival, before evening fell, Mendele stood wrapped in his prayer shawl and was about to blow the shofar, when the Gestapo officer burst into the synagogue and took him away. All the worshipers who had gathered together were frightened and started to run amok. What was the reason he had been taken? What would happen now? Why had they taken an innocent man?

Many questions gnawed at people's minds, but no one had any answers. Nobody knew.

The Gestapo officer led Mendele through the streets of the town. First of all they ordered him to take leave of his wife, who he had married just two years earlier and who was pregnant. After that they led him to the police station and from there to prison. A decree was issued forbidding anyone to be seen out on the streets of the town.

At the time I lived with a family whose father served in the Holy Society and who had the implements needed for the burial of the dead. It was a horrible night of tense anticipation, a situation of uncertainty. At four o'clock in the morning there were repeated knocks on the door, as some people requesting shovels had turned up. These were Yehiel Szrajer from Kalisz, Bram from Bydgoszcz and Bornsztajn from Jozefow. They were taken from their homes whilst still in their nightgowns, and when they got to the jail they were told: "Take this scum away from here and make him disappear in the next ten minutes, or else your fate will be the same as his."

That which their eyes saw they were unable to describe, on the ground lay Mendele, still dressed in his white Kittel, but he had been shot several times, mainly in the stomach. The man was still alive but pretended that he was dead. They were ordered to take him away and bury him immediately in the cemetery. The men lifted him up and carried him on their shoulders; on the way he begged for some water, which they gave him without anyone seeing, and when he slightly recovered, he started to talk, recounting what had happened: That evening the drunken men of the Gestapo had played a "game", put on a kind of "show" for themselves. One of the men from the Gestapo, had been bribed and had released Mendele from jail about a year earlier; he was now afraid that the witness would give him up, therefore he was prepared to say and do whatever necessary to get rid of Mendele. Mendele recognised him immediately, as "the show" which the Gestapo had organised for themselves began. They started by ordering him to do exercises: to drop to the ground and then stand up again. Then one of them shot him in the stomach, but in such a way that didn't kill him. Another shot him in the leg and then a third in the hand. In this manner they played around and abused him till morning.

The people who were carrying Mendele reached the cemetery, he was conscious the entire time. They were gripped by fear, lest they be seen not burying him. Mendele knew that he was at the cemetery; he saw the pit that they had dug for him and understood everything. He mumbled his confession and last wishes, asking that his wife not be told what had happened to him and that he had been killed in such a way, but requested that she be told that he had been transferred somewhere else. Mendele lay like this for about an hour; his white gown saturated with blood. He bled out slowly and at six o'clock in the morning they finally buried him.

The same people from the Gestapo came to the gravedigger and asked him where he had been all night. He answered that he was at home; sleeping quietly and that he knew nothing. This was corroborated by Szrajer Bram and Bornsztajn. The matter was covered up and they agreed never to talk of it. Mendele's wife guessed the truth and was stricken by insanity. The following day Mendele's grave swelled and the ground rose a little. And thus, the light of a young, innocent life was abruptly extinguished.

In February 1942, we heard by chance that the liquidation of the Jews had started in Zamosc. Some of them had been sent to an unknown place. We didn't know where to, since we were forbidden to go more than one kilometre out of Jozefow. Later more rumours reached us that Jews were no longer being transported, but that they were now killing Jews on the spot. People were unable to comprehend this and refused to believe the rumour; however, we could feel that there was truth in it and foresaw the disaster that was to come upon us.

The Gestapo from Bilgoraj, which was our town's district, came every two or three days to Jozefow. Each time that they came they had new demands and they gave us a new order; the Jews were to supply the Germans with furniture, eggs, vodka, butter, cigarettes, chocolate and all kinds of things that were not in our grasp and which were impossible to get hold of.

Luckily, there were a few families among us that received packages from abroad. We also got packages from Pola or Karla from time to time, something that helped us a lot. The Jewish Council collected whatever was left from these packages, just to shut the Germans up. Not fulfilling the decree would mean a bullet to the head.

Spring arrived; the Jews continued to go to their work places, everybody's homes were stricken by poverty and cold. Those who worked in the forests used to carry back fir tree branches on their shoulders. As evening fell every day the same scene was seen: shadows of wet and hungry people, dragging themselves home after an exhausting work day.

On 7th March 1942, the men returned home from work, as they did every day, dragging themselves back in groups. A carriage carrying members of the Gestapo arrived from the town. The Jews passed by quietly, even bowing their heads as they did so. Suddenly the carriage stopped, as the evil souls of the Gestapo must have desired some entertainment. They stopped five Jews, ordered them to put down the fir trees and lie down in a ditch. The poor men didn't know what hit them; it all happened in the blink of an eye. They lay down immediately as ordered, and those who continued to walk on heard the shots. In this manner five more new victims were scarified on the altar of German cruelty. Among those who were killed was a resident of Konin aged 32 called Cohen and four young men from Jozefow, whose names regrettably I cannot recall.

The men from the Gestapo, satisfied with their handiwork after having satisfied their killing urge, laughed and went on. The rest of us ran to the forest. The following morning, the police informed the Jewish Committee that five bodies had been found and that they needed to be removed. The dead, they claimed, had been murdered on the road and it was not known by whom. Once again, the matter was silenced.

The situation got worse from day to day. The hunger and cold did not relent, and the Gestapo and the Gendarmerie did not stop tormenting us. The Polish police also sucked our blood like leeches, as did the Polish Christian residents who helped and took part in these acts of killing and abuse.

In the town there was a young Polish man called Moniek Maszko, a butcher's son, who was also himself a butcher, he was 22 years old. Together with the Head of the Christian Community [Gielczyk], and the latter's son, Edzik, they constituted a gang of thugs that acted with no restraint. In the evenings they would raid the houses of the Jews and rape women and daughters, in front of their parents and husbands. They robbed people and stole whatever they wanted; they bit and kicked people for no reason, and this hell took place every evening. We would ask ourselves: Where would these thieves break in this evening? Whom would they beat? Who would be raped? The Jews constructed hiding places in their attics or in the cowsheds; consequently, we were able to get a few hours' sleep at night before going back to work in the mornings.

I also saw Poles who took babies and killed them by throwing them against walls.

Under these awful day-to-day conditions, Passover arrived. Anyone who had anything of value left sold it for a meagre amount of money to the Poles and bought some flour or potatoes, since we wanted to secretly bake matzos and celebrate Passover. Everyone prepared for the festival. We were promised that during the first two days of the festival we would not have to go to work and this brought us great joy; we were to receive two days of rest. At the edge of the town there had once been a Jewish bakery and it was decided to designate it for baking the matzos. This had to be done after work. From five to six o'clock in the evenings, we, the girls went to knead the dough and the men who knew how to do so, baked it in the oven.

Four days before the festival, towards evening, five or six of us were sitting together at home, when all of a sudden, the Gestapo burst in. They came to each of us and asked us our names. "No, not you!" they said, they asked us our names and then left immediately. The men jumped out of the windows and ran off. We, the women, went out the doors to the front of the house out of fear. What do they want, we asked ourselves; who are they looking for?

They burst into the neighbour's house where the Luchtfeld family lived. The father was a paralysed old man; the mother a woman now bent over from poverty and hunger; their two daughters, Bronia, who was 23 years old and Mira, who was 28 years old, both who always stood proud and erect as oaks; and their son Hunie, a strong and healthy young man. Hunie had been a soldier in the Polish army, he had made it through the war and had reached Russia, but he didn't want to leave his family without his protection and so he returns to Poland. He worked like a dog to earn them enough money for some brown bread and a bit of jam. They were a quiet and peaceful family.

We were standing in the yard, shaking like fallen leaves and our eyes followed the Germans. All of a sudden Bronia burst in shouting:

"Help! The Gestapo are beating Hunie." What had happened? Why? No one knew. They took him to another room, shouts and crying were heard, as the elderly father asked them not to beat up their son. The mother begged, not understanding what they wanted from him. The two elderly people were roughly thrown out of the room and the Gestapo continued to abuse their son. After half an hour of beatings they took him outside, to the front of the house. We stood staring out of the window at the horror that beheld our eyes and saw how they brought him out, beaten and limping. He requested that someone get him his hat that had fallen off and I handed it to him. In a weak voice he told me then why he had been beaten. One of the Volksdeutsche, who apparently still bore a grudge against Hunie going back to their time at school together, had informed on him and hoped that a bottle of vodka would be sufficient for the Gestapo to get rid of the young Jewish man.

They loaded Hunie onto a cart, and all the cries and begging didn't help. The Gestapo implied that whoever came near the cart would be shot, therefore we ran away to our respective houses. After fifteen minutes, a Polish neighbour came running out to us saying that she had heard shots. We didn't want to believe what later turned out to be the truth. We ran to the Judenrat so that they would take action and do something, but in the meantime, night had fallen and it was forbidden for us to be outside.

In the morning someone called from the police and notified us that about 2 kilometres outside the town the body of Hunie Luchtfeld was to be found. Two of his best friends buried him, not in the cemetery, since the police would not allow it. They buried him in the forest and levelled down the earth, so that no sign would be left. Four days later his brother-in-law tried to exhume the body in order to bury it clandestinely in the cemetery. He discovered that his shoes and clothes had been removed. His brother-in-law was afraid that he would draw attention to himself and in the end didn't do anything.

He knew that if he were caught, he could expect the death penalty.

1st April 1942 was the eve of Passover. The festival was marked by our sadness, grief and mourning. The two days of rest were cancelled and we had to go to work. In this manner, in a permanent state of fear from persecution and harassment by the Germans which prevailed in every corner, and especially at the hands of the Polish Head of Village [Gielczyk], his son Edzik and the infamous Moniek, the month of April passed.

Spring which had arrived could be felt outside, but everywhere people were dropping dead, swollen from hunger.

Every day at three o'clock in the afternoon, when I passed through the forest, I would see trains going by, with their wagons sealed. They were transporting Jews from France, Holland, Belgium and the Czech Republic. I knew for certain where these Jews were from because they used to look at us and call us through the barred windows. We signalled to them and showed them who we were. We wore white ribbons adorned with a blue Star of David on our arm and not the customary yellow stars on our chests and backs.

On occasion they threw postcards to us, with the questions: "Where are they taking us?" "What will they do with us?" Regrettably, we didn't have the possibility to answer them. We couldn't even get close to the wagons, as it was forbidden. On these postcards were the names of people from foreign countries, therefore we knew that Jews from these countries were also being deported and exterminated. At a later stage we discovered that they were being sent to Majdanek, Bergen-Belsen and Treblinka. It is possible that among them was my eldest sister Pola, her husband Avraham and their daughter Shulamit, who were deported from Holland around this time and no trace of them was left; only their son Yoseph (Jopie) who was saved by Dutch Christians.

During this period, we still received food packages from my sister Carla who was living in Amsterdam.

Jews were also being transported from the surrounding towns, such as: Hrubieszow, Zamosc, Bilgoraj, Tarnogrod; where to, we didn't know. Some of them were wiped out on the spot. We saw what was in store for us, but what could we do? The world was closed off to us, sealed shut and so was our fate.

1st May 1942 marked the "Workers' Festival" for the communists. They called the communists "our beloved enemies", but communism was also linked to the Jews, therefore on that morning they seized thirty-five Jews. This operation was organised by the commander of the police and by our "partner", The Master, Head of the Polish Christian Community.

To begin with, they put them in prison for a whole day without food and water, while continuously questioning them about their ties with the Russian enemy, as apparently, they were those who were helping the communists. They accused them of things that they could not even imagine. Nothing could change the outcome of the evil event that was about to take place, neither words nor money.

On the morning of 1st May, all the Jews were ordered to report to the police station at eight o'clock in the morning. We were sure that we would all be killed, but the sight we encountered froze the blood in our veins. We saw a horse driven cart, ready for departure, on which sat ten of our most revered Jewish citizens, among them were intellectuals that were accused of being communists; they said to us: "As you can see, these are our worst enemies, they have co-operated with the Russians against us. They are spies and we know what to do with them." A few of them had indeed belonged to the communist party before the war, but certainly not all of them. Just then, one of the people seated in the cart, a man called Moshe Beatus, stood up. He was a close acquaintance of mine, a teacher and a poet in the school at Konin, and we knew and could testify that he did not belong to any political organization of this or any kind, and he said: "We know where we are headed for to die for Kiddush Hashem, but

I ask that you not forget us." At that moment the horses started to gallop away.

We were all ordered to stay on the street and watch how they were being taken away by horse and cart. They knew very well that they would be killed. Towards evening they were transferred to Bilgoraj, handcuffed, and sentenced as political prisoners.

They were killed by the Germans and the Ukrainians not far from the town. We were then ordered: "Now go to work, you saw and heard nothing, woe betide he who dares speak a word."

The police commander later laughed as he told us that as soon as they had arrived in Bilgoraj they were shot in the marketplace, and warned us that this should be taken as a sign and of how one liquidates spies.

I would like to take a moment to remember a holy man, who was also among the dead - S. Anski, the ex-president of an association [Hanna could not remember which association], who was about 40 years old. This man devoted his life to science, Torah and the development of culture. When he sat in the cart, handcuffed, he said to us: "We know where we are being taken, don't forget us, we are innocent, avenge our blood." I have never forgotten them and every year on "Yom Ha'Shoa" [Holocaust Memorial Day] I light a candle in their memory.

Among them were also: Matkin from Kalisz, Maniek Markus from Rychwal, there were also some young women from Jozefow, whose names, to my regret, I cannot recall. Among the victims were also Rabbi Dembinski from Lodz and his son-in-law. The Rabbi was about 50 years old; he fled from Lodz in 1940 before the closure of the ghetto, with his wife, his daughter Fela and his other daughter and her husband. When the husbands were taken, the women decided to try and get them out at any cost, but they did not succeed. Their daughter Fela wanted to go instead of her father and said: "Let there remain a husband for my mother, take me, I am ready to die."

In the end the father was released, but they refused to release their son-in-law, and his wife went with him of her own free will. They were supposed to take them half way and then send them back, but regrettably, they shot them along the way, and the commander of the police took whatever he found on their bodies and in their possession for his only daughter who was about to get married the next month.

Rabbi Dembinski and his wife were tormented by their conscience because they knew their children had gone to their deaths in order to save them. They were stricken with madness. The Rabbi's wife used to walk among her acquaintances, imploring them: "Please, tell me, our children are alive, right?" She even went to the police commander, who stood for all that was bad, wicked and cruel, and who was thirsty for Jewish blood. He took the last ring the broken mother, whose heart was in anguish, had, promising that he would ensure that at least the girls would be released. Have you ever seen a dead person come back from the grave? And so, they too never returned.

From this moment on we felt like nothing. Any Pole, Ukrainian and of course member of the SS, could do whatever they wished with us. Many of the young people ran away to the forests and joined the partisans, and others escaped in other ways.

Again, we had a few days of quiet, if it is possible to call them this. For seven or eight days there were no victims; therefore, we called them quiet days.

One good thing happened in Jozefow, Ida and Anton (Arie) Piotrowski got married on the 3rd of February 1942.

On 10th May a big Aktzia took place. At five o' clock in the morning there were knocks at the door. At the front door stood the Police Commander and the Head of the Christian Community, they pushed me aside and barged into the room. My brother [Yehudah] understood, in the blink of an eye what was happening and he jumped out of the window. They shot at him in order to stop him but, they didn't catch him, and he managed to escape. They took father. The commander wanted to shoot him there and then with his pistol. I burst out crying and so did mother, for some reason it touched his heart. They also took the landlord from the second room in the house. We could already see what was happening, so with only a shirt to my body I snuck out through the fence. It was night, dogs were barking, terror was everywhere, shouts and cries could be heard from the town. There were knocks at the window; I didn't know what to do. Who could I approach to ask for help? And where was my brother?

I ran to my sister Ida's house. There on the granary floor lay my brother and my sister's husband Anton, shaking with fear, but this was not enough, I knew we also had to save father. If we did not save him at the start of the panic, later it would be too late. Not far from us lived the Chairman of the Judenrat, Goralnik from Konin. We ran to him as fast as we could and he asked us what had happened. Before we managed to say a word, all of a sudden there were knocks at the door as the police had arrived. Goralnik jumped out the window with my sister, his wife and I got into bed and covered ourselves. "Where is your husband?" asked the Police Commander? He has to present himself tomorrow at ten o'clock, he said and then he was gone. Well then, what next? We asked ourselves after he had gone. Goralnik had run to the forest, we ran to Majzels, the second Judenrat representative, but here again we faced bad luck, as the police arrived immediately after us. Maizels didn't manage to escape, he was beaten on the spot and they took him. When we saw that the abductions included everyone, we ran to warn a few more families so that the men would have sufficient time to run away and hide.

In the morning we found out that there was a decree for a quota of 180 Jews. The Germans were already exempt from dealing with this, so the Poles took it upon themselves to execute this Aktzia. During this time young men aged 17-18 took advantage of the situation and raided Jewish houses, looting anything they wanted from them.

The decree by the Bilgoraj Gestapo was for 180 Jews, but the Poles gathered 300. They took, women, men, young girls, young boys without any discrimination, what a horror. In the prison there was only room for 60 people, but they pushed in 300. A trade in human beings began, who would be released and for what ransom?

The poor incarcerated people sat in the prison for twenty-four hours, suffocating from lack of air to breathe, any access or contact with them was denied. Around the prison the Polish youth stood guard so that no one could escape, so that no "Parsziwi Zid" [A common Polish anti-Semitic curse meaning: A Jew stricken by boils and leprosy] would get away from there.

The first to be released was Maizels who was a member of the Judenrat, the head of the Christian Community gave his consent to this. In order to release father and one more person, we paid thirty dollars, the rest of the money that we had left, which had been hidden and was being kept for the right moment. We had managed to transfer the money in our intestines, and at the time of the search in Lodz they hadn't discovered that we had money. There was joy in our house as we celebrated father's release.

However, in the town the terrible events did not cease. I saw how a resident of Jozefow called Kalksztajn, lost his son, aged 17, who was taken that night. The father of the young man asked that he be exchanged for his elderly grandfather and the head of the Christian Community agreed. The father, Kalksztajn, dragged his elderly father to exchange him for his son, who had been taken to his certain death, and he said to him: "Father you are very old and my son is still young, you have to die first". The old man, who was 70 years old, adorned with a white patriarchal beard, was led to the prison, as he mumbled to himself: "I know where I am headed, but I am already old, and the world belongs to the young." After an hour his son was released, but this did not prevent the killing of both the father and the son at a later stage.

I saw how Mrs. Kawalek parted from her only son, Majrus, who was only 23. He was condemned to death by Mundzik because he was an invalid; and why was he an invalid? Because he had fought in the lines of the Polish army to free the Poles, during which time Mundrzjk had stolen and gotten rich at the expense of the Jews.

I saw how two young boys aged 16 or 17 lynched a Jew called Zelkowicz from Konin. Zelkowicz was fifty years old. He was a sculptor. Why?

We saw scenes such as these on everywhere. Any Pole would take whatever could be taken or stolen from the Jews. This was a terrifying day, where neither law nor justice prevailed.

The Commander of the Polish Police and the Head of the Christian Community, who were Poles, took bribes from anyone that they could. But what were they to do with the people who were above the quota? Arendowski came and took fifty people to work in his sawmill, a few more were ransomed for money, and thus they were left with 180 victims who were destined to be turned over to the Gestapo.

This Aktzia continued until ten o'clock in the morning. The Gestapo arrived, drunk as usual. It was a market day in the town; people were going back and forth and whispering that Jews would be killed today. The poor victims, who were destined to be murdered, were not taken out of the sight of their loved ones and the killings took place in front of their horrified eyes.

Firstly, they took 25 of them and gave them shovels. They were ordered and forced to dig ditches about one kilometre long outside the town. When they had finished digging the ditches, the other 155 Jews that were in the prison, under the command of the Gestapo, were taken by Mundzik and Edzik and all the riotous gang, who made them run through the streets of the town, beating and kicking them as soon as they came out of the prison.

Among them was a person called Bas, from Konin, who was about

40 years old. He was a blind invalid, and he was lynched as soon as he left the prison. They beat him with sticks, since he was unable to go as fast and keep up with the others. Mundzik took Majrus' crutches from him and beat him to death with them, watching him fall to the ground.

There were others who tried to escape, like Josef Frenkel from Skulsk [The brother of Shulem Frenkel], aged 30, and Boas Grabinski from Slesin, also aged 30. The Gestapo shot them in the leg, so that they would not die immediately and later they buried them alive.

From the prison to the point of execution it was about one kilometre. All along this path the earth was saturated with blood. Decapitated heads rolled, parts of torn limbs, hands here, feet there, all of innocent victims. The rest were shot with machine guns and the Poles buried them.

The young people who heard what had happened ran away to hiding places in order to try and take cover there. We understood what was in store for us.

But the Gestapo's thirst for blood was probably not satisfied, as they returned full of wrath before the evening and took more Jews from their houses and murdered them.

The Poles were those who pointed out the Jewish houses, themselves taking out Jews to the front of their houses and murdering them on the spot. In this way, Heine Ajman Czadek from the town of Slesin, the mother of two toddlers was murdered. She was unable to run away since her children were sick and her husband was away at work. They took her out in front of the shed she was living in; all the yells and cries of the children and their mother did not move them at all, and they shot her like a dog. The horrified children were found lying next to their mother's body yelling, "Mama." Their father returned the following day to find this scene and the poor man had to carry on living for the sake of his children.

Similarly, they murdered a woman called Szajna Bresler from

Skulsk, aged about 50; she was also murdered in front of her children. Edzik grabbed her by her hair and dragged her to the front of the house; before we could say a word, a shot was heard. Again, the life of a woman, the mother of four children, was viciously taken.

The drunken police and Gestapo called the Judenrat and ordered them to deliver goods to them within the hour: ten litres of vodka, fifty eggs, one kilogram of cocoa, one kilogram of coffee and three kilograms of butter; and if these were not delivered to them: "You know what to expect from previous cases", they threatened.

Where would we get coffee? Where would we get cocoa in a small Ukrainian town where all its people resources had already been exhausted? Bread was a scarce product and even a potato was far off dream. But the shortage did not bother the Gestapo, they didn't care at all. On the contrary, a life-threatening order could not be ignored. So what were we to do?

While we were lying low in the forests and mountains, shivering with cold and fear, the Jews in the town started to go from door to door, gathering food, gram by gram from the little which people had kept hidden for the right time, really for medicinal purposes. People gave whatever bribes they could in order to calm the animalist instincts of the murderers of mothers, children and our brothers. This went on for the entire night, until the task was completed.

On the following days, on our way to work, those of us who were left saw the burial mounds on the side of the road moving and shifting since they had buried alive the people that they had tortured and beaten to death, and whose souls had not yet left them. The burial mounds swelled. Later the young men reburied the dead and straightened out the mounds.

The situation became more sever and deteriorated from day to day; we felt that all of us would soon be killed. Those Jews who did manage to escape unnoticed by the Germans were often given up by the Poles and consequently discovered. For each Jew that the Poles gave up they would receive half a kilogram of sugar; this was the price for the life of a Jew. Every last one of them knew that they were delivering us to certain, agonizing, and death at the hands of the Germans. Parents gave their children to strangers, mainly to Poles, in exchange for a suitable fee, since they knew that they themselves were lost in any event; but after a week or two those same treacherous Poles exposed them and handed them over to the Germans. The atmosphere all over Poland was abominably hostile towards the Jews and our situation was desperate.

People started to look for any means, way and ruse to escape and assimilate into the Christian population all over Poland, without having their Jewish origin exposed. A new "industry" of forging documents started to evolve. Every other family started to prepare "Kennkarte", forged identity cards, for its members. These documents were sold by a local Pole who had a dubious "reputation" as being the greatest murderer in the area, in addition to being a drunkard, robber and a thief. These were the hands in which we put our lives. In the evenings he would secretly come to our homes, bringing with him a written document, ready and completed - a certificate the same as those which the Poles had - using the name of a stranger on it, a Pole who had died or was missing. We, on our part, gave him a photo and our finger prints. For this piece of paper, which was supposed to save our lives, we were willing to give him whatever we had left: a dress, a suit or a coat, if any of these were still left in anyone's possession. However, these were not considered good merchandise, he wanted gold, dollars, diamonds - these were the goods with which it was possible to buy the Kennkarte.

Everybody was caught up in the business of purchasing papers; women, both young and old, and men of all ages. Some of them had a typical "Jewish look", but no one gave any consideration to this matter or to the fact that they might in fact endanger others by giving them away as well. Everyone held fast onto the last anchor of salvation - Polish papers.

Consequently, dozens of people perished, since only those who had Polish features succeeded in somehow integrating into the surrounding and living amongst the Poles. Those who escaped as Poles to the nearby towns and villages and were then caught, were forced to divulge how they had gotten their papers and by doing so put others in jeopardy.

Yaakov: In spite of the difficult situation, father, who had a great will to live wanted to survive; therefore, he went into hiding. Mother couldn't take it anymore; she couldn't tolerate the insult and the humiliation, and she decided that she preferred to die. She wore the most beautiful clothes that she still had and left the house; she volunteered to go to her death. My mother, the most gentle, noble, beautiful woman, put into practice the words:" Now, O Jehovah, please take away my life, for it is better for me to die than to live."

Hanna: When both of us were still at home mother tried to speak to my heart and convince me that I should come with her in the upcoming Aktzia. "What reason is there for living this kind of life?" she said to me. But I answered: "Mother, I am still young and I want to live."

On 10th July 1942, 20 Jewish men were taken by the police in Jozefow to dig pits outside the town in the adjacent forest, next to the cemetery. Later those same 20 men who were selected were forced to go into the pit and they were covered with lime, another 20 people were then forced into the pit and the same action was repeated. They said that it was a pity to waste bullets on Jews. After this story, the streets were full of people looking for any possible way to escape; they did not manage to do so and they were all murdered immediately.

It was the Poles who gathered the victims and brought them to the forest, to the threshold of the pits, where the SS, while drunk, shot them with machine guns and watched as they fell into the pits. Mother was killed immediately, but not all of the victims died immediately, some of them fell into the pit alive. Later the Germans sent the Poles and the Ukrainians to finish the job and said to them: "Kill everyone who is still alive, and don't let anyone escape." The Ukrainians beat whoever had survived, smashed their heads in with the butts of their rifles and killed them, saying: "It's a pity to waste bullets on Jews." In this manner, all of them were killed and buried, until the very last Jew who was caught. They covered them with lime and waited to execute the next layer. In this Aktzia 350 Jews were murdered.

In the same Aktzia, Pola Gliksman, Yaakov's girlfriend, who was 20 years old, and her mother Dora from Skulsk, were also caught. After the shooting they remained alive. Pola's foot was badly hurt from the shooting. After the Germans left, they crawled out of the pit. Pola begged the Polish young men who were in charge of the burial: "Please let us run to the forest, the German police will not notice", but they beat them to death with shovels and hoes. After they did this, they boasted about it.

Yaakov: Father and a few other Jews who were in hiding managed to survive and were caught later; they were ordered to gather the corpses and bury them. Among the corpses they identified mother, and also Pola Gliksman and her mother Dora. They buried them all. Father said "Kaddish", cried and said; "I am not crying for the dead but for those who are still alive, their death is better than our lives".

After this event father gathered all of us and said to us: "You, who are young, run away in all directions, I have already lived my life." Father gave us his blessing, we separated, and with the forged documents we started to escape, each of us going to a different place.

Hanna: On 13th July 1942, at seven o'clock in the morning, the Jews of Jozefow were ordered to report to a certain place, they gathered most of the Jews that were still left in Jozefow and in the same manner as described above killed and murdered them.

But not all the Jews presented themselves, some of them hid. This time our bitter enemies went from house to house, looking in all the cellars and other hiding places; if anybody was found, man, woman or child, they were murdered on the spot. The streets, the forest and the houses, all spilled over with corpses. Outside the town, horrible tragedies took place again. 25 machine guns were positioned there and all the Jews who had been gathered were shot. Those who were not killed immediately by the bullets were beaten to death by axes and shovels. The killings continued from eight o'clock in the morning until midnight. The Gestapo and the German Order Police were those who drenched their hands in this blood. They travelled to the town and brought in additional victims. The Poles handled the digging and the burying of corpses. [The members of Reserve Police Battalion 101 of Hamburg had been brought to Jozefow during the night between the 12th and 13th of July, from their nearby base in Bilgoraj and they performed the killings. The corpses were not covered and remained on the ground, only at a much later stage were the remains collected and buried in mass graves in the forest. This was the last massacre in Jozefow.]

The Rogorzynski family, Gabrisz's family, was in Jozefow too. They reached Jozefow together with us when we were exiled from Skulsk. When I disguised myself as a Polish village woman and left for the railway station, I met Gabrisz's two sisters, Sala and Tamar, who were on their way back from work. Sala asked me: "Hanna, are you running away?" I answered, "Yes." These were the last words that I exchanged with them. On that night, all of the Rogorzinski family from my town; three sisters, two brothers and their parents were executed. Not a person was left from Gabrisz's family, except Gabrisz himself, who immigrated to the Land of Israel in 1936.

On the same night, all those left from the Shulem Frenkel family, my friends from Skulsk, were also killed, except for Shulem himself who was in hiding and was not discovered. When Shulem came out from his hiding place in the morning, it being a miracle that he was still alive, he saw the "City of Slaughter", as Chaim Nachman Bialik described it: "The sun was shining and the slaughterer slaughtered." Only it was not just the slaughterer, but the whole world that saw how we were being slaughtered and stood by silent… Shulem found his dead mother, where she had already "fallen prey to the cats" in the garbage bin. She was alone, and he brought her to burial in a field, without anybody seeing him.

On that night, the Gestapo, having quenched their thirst for blood by that which had already been spilt, and tired after a whole day of killings, stopped shooting people. They simply started to bury people alive. In this way, saturated in blood, the women of the Bigos family from Skulsk, a mother and two daughters, one aged 23 and the other aged15, rose out of their grave. They had been on top of all the others who were in the pit and had by some miracle survived. The criminals who had dealt with the work of killing and burying the dead were ine-briated by vodka, and maybe because of this they were saved. When the Gestapo and the gravediggers departed, they waited for an hour and then came out of the mass grave and ran to the forest.

The following morning, disguised as Polish farm women, they ran to Ostrowiec Kielecki. There the Jews had not been annihilated in this way yet, but at a later stage the Germans found them and they were also murdered.

That night was the grand finale, the annihilation of the Jews of my small town Skulsk, and the Jews of the towns of Slesin, a few from Kalisz, Konin, Rychwal and Grodziec and of course from Jozefow itself. On that night at least one 1500 Jews were killed in Jozefow. I have not forgotten them…

I was told about what happened on that day, 13th July 1942, by my brother [Yehudah], who had escaped from Jozefow that night, and by another woman called Bigos, who had also survived and corrobo-rated it in writing from Ostrowiec. I was already out of Jozefow; this massacre happened eight days after my arrival at Cichoborz.

Growing up I had spent more time in Sompolno than in my own home. I had a grandmother, grandfather, uncles, aunts and many cousins there. In Sompolno there had thrived a positive Jewish youth, educated and full of life.

When the Germans entered Sompolno in September 1939, the Jews suffered from all the "customary" persecutions: confiscation of property, limitation of movement, forced labour, wearing of the yellow star, torture and humiliation. On the ninth of the month of Av, 1941, the Jews were concentrated in the town square and after being checked by a German officer for their fitness to work, the first group of town's men were taken to forced labour camps in the Poznan area. Two days later an additional group was sent off to the labour camps.

The brutal persecution worsened and the possibility for the rest of the Jews of the town to escape the restricted zone was prevented. In the end the Jews of Sompolno were not deported. On 2nd February 1942, the Germans surrounded Sompolno and entered the town with great forces. They loaded about 1000 of the town's Jews onto trucks and transported them to the extermination camp in Chelmno. The Germans killed them in "Gas Vans", which had air-tight compartments for victims, into which exhaust fumes were diffused while the engine was left running. Later they buried them in layers in pits; on top of each layer they covered the bodies with lime. Part of the Wilczynski and Sompolinski families perished in Chelmno. The survivors of Sompolno were those who survived the forced labour camps.

[When Efri visited Poland in 2003, he met Zigmunt Nasielski, a native of Skulsk, then in his eighties. They visited Chelmno together and there Zigmunt, who was an eye witness to what had happened, told him that at the burial sites, in the mass graves, the earth had moved and shifted up and down for two to three days because some of the murdered people were still alive when they were buried. Later the Poles were ordered by the Germans to level off the earth.]

"On the Day of Their Death"

[This song was written originally in Yiddish in rhyme.]

And God blessed that day with grace
The sun shone in all its glory just for spite
The forest stood alone, silence all around
And the sound of the birds singing was heard in all its grandeur

Softly moved the many weeds
Quietly whispered the daily prayer
The trees dreamt in the peaceful forest,
Still, how beautiful was the idyllic scene

Suddenly the forest shuddered in panic,
The birds stopped their singing all at once
What had happened?
The world had never seen anything like it

Roaring vehicles, shots are heard
Innocent Jewish blood already spilt
Rifles making an incessant noise
The Gestapo running around, blood thirsty like hungry jackals

The green field had already turned red
From every direction only murder and death dominated
New victims brought from all over
Quickly Jews, cover the moribund with earth

Thousands of Jews, like moving sands
Killed by his cruel hand
Mothers and toddlers together
At the same forest's edge

As a raging tempest
So, with speed they were taken
From the bosom of each mother
They tore away the children to their deaths

Every mother was forced to see
How each father dug a grave
As every limb of his trembled
A grave for his children

Why, precisely when my people bled
? Did you, the sun, shine with brightest light
Nature blossomed in all its glorious beauty
? Why did the light of day not turn into night

! Oh God, think for just a moment
? What have you done to your people
You gave he who hates you all the power
In spite of his ridicule for you and your people

: And God replied
This was my command"

I do not recognise you as my people
Your guilt is too great - you have sinned too much

Your suffering will continue
You will not have a minute of peace
But days will come
When evil will change to good

The day will come and an end to the murderers will come
But not soon - it will still take some time
And then I shall judge them
And completely annihilate their country and their people."

And today I am standing orphaned over your graves
And every limb of mine is weeping and raging inside me
Of these things I shall pour out my heart, and because of them
my soul cries
Here! This is the binding of my people on the mountain of Moriah

Sleep peacefully in your graves our dear parents
We, the sons, are already creating a new world
How terrible that your innocent lives were taken from you
The enemy will have no hope when you rise at the resurrection

The red flag has won and is waving gloriously;
For you and for every one of our dead
The enemy has been wiped out for ever, from its very foundation,
terrible is the vengeance
And for us who have remained, how great is the comfort

Yaakov Kotowski 11 December 1945

The Escapes

Hanna: In April 1942, my brother Yaakov escaped to a village called Cichoborz, situated near the city of Hrubieszow, about ninety kilometres from Jozefow. At the time the poverty in Jozefow was unbearable, there was terrible hunger, disease, in addition to the abuse, harassment and the Aktzias. We had an immense will to live; therefore, we decided to escape, by impersonating Poles and moving to other places where we would look for work in order to make a living. Yaakov, who did not have a Jewish look, bought forged documents to get out of Jozefow and left to look for work. He understood and took advantage of the opportunity in time, when the matter of faking Polish documents was still not so widespread. He moved away to work as an agronomist on a big farm that belonged to an estate-owning Pole who was part of the Polish nobility, and he was far from Jozefow. He had learnt this profession before the war on Hakhsharah, when he planned to go to the Land of Israel. He was well educated and spoke Polish fluently. While working for this Paritz he earned the appreciation of both his employer and of all the other workers.

Yaakov: We worked for the Germans in the forests, under forced labour. It was hard and exhausting work, under unbearable conditions, impossible to describe. And when Damocles' sword hovered above us, I called out to my friends and pleaded with them to stop being indifferent to their fate and to try and save themselves: "Wake up, wake up young men of Israel, our people are dying." Save yourselves! The only thing we have left to lose are our chains of subjugation, and maybe there is still a chance, even if it is slim, that we may win back our freedom and our lives. Ha! Ha! Who can live together with these Polish and Ukrainian philistines? But nobody listened to me. "And no one got up like the lion, or moved as would the lion's cub; no one in the town cried out." I remained a lone voice crying out. I sold my last shirt and bought a Polish identity card from one Adam Kowalski, of Rychwal. When I left Jozefow I was no longer Yaakov Kotowski; he gave me a new name, Ciszewski Jan. I ran away from the bleeding town of Jozefow as fast as I could, to a small town called Cichoborz, which is located near a city called Hrubieszow.

The Baron Pohorecki Jackowski was a big Polish Paritz who was the owner of a few manor houses. He took me to work on his farm as a dairy farmer. At a later stage he sent me on a course so that I would learn how to manage his dairy and meat production on the farm, after which he appointed me Head Milkman.

In my capacity as the person responsible for all the dairy and meat of the Paritz, which was very important to the Germans during the time of the war, I was appointed by the Gestapo as an essential senior clerk and they made sure to grant me documents that enabled me to travel all over Poland without limitation.

Hanna: Yaakov didn't witness what we did in Jozefow up until the month of July. However, the fate of the Jews in his area was no different. We wrote to him under a fabricated name. Our situation deteriorated from day to day and when he heard about what was happening in Jozefow he wrote back to me telling me to come to Cichoborz and be with him, in the same way that he had escaped. In one of the letters that I received from him he wrote that the wife of the accountant in Cichoborz, Mrs. Kotulewicz, was looking for somebody to help her, because she was getting old.

To begin with I didn't want to leave my parents and so I waited.

In addition, by this time, in July 1942, leaving Jozefow was very dangerous and punishable by death. Guards of the Order Police were posted in all directions around the town; supposedly they were there as a defence against the partisans, but at that time there weren't any partisans in the area.

My sister Ida and her husband Anton Piotrowski had also bought forged papers and left in this way, they went to work in Germany as Polish Christians. My brother Yehudah also bought forged papers and planned to pass over to the "Aryan" side.

I too bought a scrap of paper to get me out, in exchange for my dear mother's wedding ring, the last valuable thing that we had left. By this stage, there was severe poverty at home, and outside there was nothing but hunger and extermination of Jews all over the place. I felt that the end was getting nearer. There were executions every day, killings from morning till night, still I didn't want to leave, and I didn't want to be separated from my parents. There was a rumour that the SS and the Poles intended to liquidate all the Jews in Jozefow, the town was full of policemen. I

was ready for this situation with my forged papers.

On the night of 2nd July 1942, I dressed up in the clothes of a provincial woman and covered my head with a scarf. I took leave of my parents with an aching heart and tearful eyes, since I knew that I would never ever see them again. My father blessed me before I left. I was going to escape from Jozefow, a town of the walking dead. I headed for the railway station at 7 o'clock in the morning together with all the labourers who were leaving for work, as if I was one of them. I left for the unknown and knew that it was possible that I was heading for my death, but by this time I didn't have anything to lose.

When I reached the railway station, the one closest to the town, the place was swarming with policemen. The police were scrutinising everyone's faces. At every station they were looking deep into the eyes of the travellers, checking how they behaved and following their reactions, like animals hunting for their prey, since it was a well-known fact that Jews were trying to pass through clandestinely with forged papers.

I approached a woman and told her that I wasn't feeling well and asked her to buy me a train ticket to Cichoborz. It was a great risk, she could have taken the money and not bought me a ticket, but she did and I boarded the train.

On the train everybody was talking about the Jews and I heard some who said: "It is good that they are being liquidated" and "It's about time to finish them off." Surrounded by this atmosphere I travelled for twenty four hours, until finally I reached Cichoborz. In this way I left for a new life; full of Jewish blood, I started over with a new name: "Anna (Hanka) Kotecka."

When I reached Cichoborz I passed from house to house looking for work. The people were good but wretchedly poor; eventually I reached the house of the accountant's wife, and she received me with open arms. She had a nice house. She had a son who studied in Lublin. I became their housemaid. I started to accompany the lady of the house on her errands, I did the shopping for her, and other things that she couldn't do alone. I helped her with everything.

My life changed beyond recognition; it started to take a normal course, but in spite of everything I had many sleepless nights, since I feared that I might speak Yiddish while dreaming.

Cichoborz was a large and rich town; it was in the surroundings of the city of Hrubieszow, which was not far from the city of Lublin. My brother Yaakov worked in Cichoborz on a large, rich and beautiful estate, under the alias: Jan (Janusz) Ciszewski. I didn't know his new name before I came to the town. The town was surrounded by large intertwined forests. The place was quiet, as if the war hadn't reached it. There, life went on as usual, without any problems. The Manor House owner was the Baron Pohorecki, who lived with his wife, son and daughter, all of whom were educated people. The baron was a wise man and elegant in his external appearance. The children were from his first marriage. His second marriage was to a woman many years younger than himself. The relationship between the children and the stepmother was not good, and everybody knew it. But the baron, who was a good man, was deeply loved by the town's people and his relationship with them was such that no one talked about this subject. In addition, politics, and the problems of the Jews, did not interest him or the members of his family.

On the estate lived a couple of old Jews who had two sons. They worked on the baron's pear tree plot. One day the Polish police came and took their sons, I didn't know where to or why. The baron asked the Germans to leave the old couple alone and promised that they would not get involved in politics, and that he would be responsible for them. I always kept my distance from them, since I was afraid that they would identify me as a Jewess.

Days would pass by and I wouldn't see my brother Yaakov. In the town I knew the young people who worked for the baron and we would spend time together. Cichoborz was like an isolated island, and far from the real world, and this was also the reason that information about the bitter events happening all over Poland did not reach our ears.

One evening, during one of the dances that took place there, my brother Yaakov and I met by chance and we behaved as if we were complete strangers, meeting there for the first time. We pretended to fall in love and become a couple. It was possible since we had different names.

As we were considered a couple, I met my brother on many occasions. We wandered around with other young people, danced and enjoyed good things. Everybody loved Yaakov, who was then known as Janusz. He had a cheerful disposition and knew how to play the viola well; when he played the other young people would join him singing and dancing. Everybody thought that we were going to get married. When we were on our own, we would often talk about the situation the world was in, since we knew everything that was going on from the radio.

One time I was dancing with one of the young men while my brother was playing the viola, and then he said to me: "Hanka look! This Janusz guy looks like a Jew playing in a synagogue." I burst out laughing and said: "I have never been to a synagogue and I don't know how Jews play."

Every day I would go to the village to bring four litres of milk for Mrs Kotulewicz, the woman that I worked for. Due to her husband's job she was entitled to it.

It was a wonderful day and it was morning time. I went for a walk in the Baron's Family Park, on the way I sat down on a bench and started to think about my life. I was waiting for the cows to return from the pasture. Suddenly, I felt somebody touch my shoulder. I turned around and saw the old Jewish woman from the estate standing behind me. She blessed me and asked: "Madam, do you know what day it is today?" I said: "Monday or Tuesday". "No", said the old lady and started crying: "Today is a great day for us Jews, today is Yom Kippur."

Immediately, I could picture my parents' house, my mother dressed for the festival holding the Siddur in her hand and my father dressed in his white Kittel. I saw us; five daughters dressed in white from top to bottom, our dresses starch ironed, and three sons, with Kippahs on their heads, all waiting for father to bless us before he left for the synagogue. For a moment I didn't know where I was.

The old lady stared at me in wonder and said: "What's wrong Madam?" I was scared that I would start crying and answered: "No, Madam, I don't know what Yom Kippur is, since I never had any Jewish acquaintances." Then I stood up intentionally and said: "The cows are coming back from the fields; I have to go since Mrs Kotulewicz is waiting for me."

The old woman went on her way, and I was left by myself, afraid someone may have seen me talking to her.

That night I met my confidant, my brother Yaakov, and asked him if he knew what day it was. I told him that it was Yom Kippur. Neither of us joked around that night.

At a later stage, the police took the old couple as well and executed them not far from the estate.

Our brother Yehudah, as already mentioned also ran away using forged papers. His alias was Juzik Kotecki. He lived in another Manor House, in a different village not far from us. Since both of us had the same name - Kotecki - we said that we were cousins and he used to come to visit us from time to time, as my cousin. In this way I could receive him in Mrs. Kotulewich's house. He worked like anybody else and at that time, had a good life. We lived like this for about a year and it seemed that we could go on like this till the end of the war, but destiny has its own will and destiny wanted it to be otherwise.

Yaakov: My sister Hanna arrived in Cichoborz not long after me, and both of us lived there as an engaged Polish couple. Every Sunday we would go together to pray at church. We started to "forget" that we were Jews. Hanna got work as a housemaid at the Kotulewicz family; the head of the family was an accountant. She helped Mrs. Kotulewicz with all the household chores; she did the laundry, took care of the pigs and did all that a servant in Poland did in those days. It was exhausting work. After work Hanna used to come and eat with me, since at Mrs Kotulewich's she was always hungry and at my place there was no shortage of food.

However, when the Paritz saw us taking walks together on the estate's boulevard, on more than one occasion he said to me: "Sir, how come your fiancée looks so much like you?" I, being scared stiff would laugh it off and told him that it only seemed so to him. The last thing we needed was for the ignoramus to figure out that this was in fact the truth.

My brother Yehudah, who had also escaped from Jozefow lived on a Manor House too, but in another village called Husynne, which was not far away. He held a senior position; he was in charge of a big warehouse belonging to a German business, on a German farm. I was afraid to keep in touch with him, so we seldom met. Yehuda worked there with a childhood friend of ours called Edek Bialystocki.

Hanna: One day I went for a walk, as I was in the habit of doing, and I met the Baron, the Manor House owner. He talked to me politely and asked me about myself and about my family, and if I felt welcome at the house of Mrs. Kotulewicz. Of course, I replied that everything was fine and that I felt happy at Mrs. Kotulewicz's house. He then added: "I hear that you are Ciszewski's girlfriend, isn't it odd how alike you both look?" I thought that the earth had opened wide under my feet and that soon it would swallow me alive, I laughed it off and told him that he must be mistaken and hurried home.

That night I met with my brother Yaakov and I told him everything that had happened with the Baron. Both of us decided that it would be best if I left the estate as soon as possible. But what would I do? Where would I go?

A few days passed, and then I told Mrs. Kotulewicz that I didn't love Janusz anymore, that the relationship between us was over, and that I would like to leave. At the same time, I wrote a letter to my sister Ida, who lived in the city of Dresden in Germany with her husband Anton, and I asked her opinion about what I should do.

Yaakov playing the violin. The elderly woman and the accordi-
onist are from same family. The two women on her left and right
are Jewish women from Warsaw. The man with the moustache
is Jan Gorski, Hanna's neighbour. Cichoborz 20.06.1942

The Spy

Yaakov: At that time, many young Poles started to assemble in the forests for a partisan war against the Germans. They used to steal arms from the warehouses of the Germans and then fight them, especially from within the forests. During the day, the Polish partisans would work on the farms which were in the villages, but at night they fought. The whole area was occupied by a great deal of German forces, who were incessantly chasing the Polish partisans.

Since I spoke some German, and the Germans had appointed me as a senior clerk for them, I used my position and proximity to them to penetrate the ranks of the Gestapo. Simultaneously I joined the Polish partisans and I spied for them. In this manner, during the day I would listen to the conversations of the Germans and at night I would run and inform the Polish partisans what the Germans' plans were. Then, the partisans would foil these plans causing the Germans to pay a heavy price.

Since the economic situation in Germany was dire, the Germans exploited the Polish farms until the very end. They gained control of all their agricultural production; 90% was sent to Germany and the remaining 10% was used for local consumption. This enraged the Poles deeply.

The Germans are notorious for being meticulous and they measured everything very accurately. For instance, on the dairy farm they would check how much milk was produced each day, how much milk had to be given to the calves, how much was used to make butter and cheese, and then they would send the rest to Germany as per their calculations.

I, being the Head Milkman, was responsible for the dairy farming on the estate; but in spite of their meticulous calculations, I always had some surplus. How did I manage this? I would add some groats to the milk that the calves received, thus making the milk thicker and the calves would be satisfied faster. In this way, I was left with the surplus. I would prepare butter and cheeses and give some to the Germans to send to their families, since in those days there was still a shortage of food in Germany. They were very pleased with me and this was how I won them over and became their "friend".

Since I was their friend, I was in close proximity to them on more than one occasion during the day. They discussed their plans against the Polish partisans amongst themselves in my presence. I would listen and pass on this sensitive information to the partisans. Whenever I sat among them, my body trembled and the blood in my veins froze, for I knew that if they suspected for even a moment that I was a Jew or a spy, they would have killed me on the spot or send me to the death camps.

As a result of the information that I supplied to the Polish partisans, they would prepare themselves accordingly. They would surround the location where the Germans had gathered to set out on a mission, forming a "suffocation ring" around them, thus dealing them a heavy blow. Following an operation such as this the Germans naturally suffered heavy casualties.

The Poles hated the Germans immensely and tortured them whenever they could. After a battle like this, whoever they didn't kill they took hostage, but they didn't keep the Germans in captivity. They would hang them up by their legs from the trees in the forests, with their heads touching the ground on a red ants nest. In the forests of Poland there were red ants, each the size of half a toe, and they were carnivorous. They would leave them hanging like this and return a week later to find only their skeletons left.

I participated in battles with the partisans on several occasions. Luckily, the Germans never saw me and therefore didn't suspect me. The Germans were going out of their minds. They knew that there was a spy among them, but they couldn't figure out who it was. They took such heavy losses in the area that eventually they gave up and just after 6 months they retreated from Cichoborz and its surroundings and left for the district capital, Hrubieszow.

The Polish partisans didn't know that I was a Jew, if they had known they would have killed me or immediately handed me over to the Germans and this in spite of the fact that I continuously risked my life for them; they were anti-Semitic from birth, they suckled anti-Semitism from their mother's milk. But they suspected me and they had good reason to. They liked to get drunk, and I was not used to it; I didn't like it and I was always careful not to do so, since to lose my self-control for even a moment would have meant to risk my life. Another custom that was common among the Poles was that they used to go to the urinals together; a thing that could reveal my identity immediately since I was circumcised, therefore I never went to the urinals with them.

The Paritz Pohorecki also suspected that I was a Jew. I took such good care of the dairy farm that he said to me more than once that he thought I was a Jew. "Only a Jewish mind can do what you do for the dairy farm" he said. Of course, I laughed and told him that this wasn't true, but he was a good man by nature and I was not afraid that he would turn me in to the Germans.

Majdanek -
The Blessing and the Testament

Yaakov: After the big massacre in Jozefow on 13th July 1942 the Germans started to send those who were still alive to the extermination camps. Father was sent to the extermination camp of Majdanek near Lublin. In this transport were also the Rabbi of our town, Beatus, and the rest of our town's people.

I used my position, having documents which allowed me to travel without limitation all over Poland, and I reached Majdanek. It was the eve of "Shavuot" [the Pentecost Festival], which occurred on 8th June 1943]; the acacia bloomed, the lilac blossomed, the sun shone and the slaughterer slaughtered. On this day I entered the lion's den, the extermination camp of Majdanek, disguised as a Polish peddler selling haberdashery items, in order to part from my father, just a single day before he was led to the gas chambers, his body later to be burnt in the fiery furnace [crematorium].

He put his scrawny, shaking hands on my head in order to bless me. He cried, as the droplets of his boiling tears flowed from his eyes wetting my head, and which I can feel to this very day, as he said to me: "Get out my son, see your electrocuted friends on the barbed wire fences that surround the camp." Then he asked his last request of me: My first strength, Aharon Leib, is no longer among the living. You, my youngest son and your brother Yehudah are still alive. Disperse, so our family will not be obliterated.

And the following is the most precious blessing that my father ever gave me, just a day before his dead body entered the fiery furnace: "Listen my son to the blessing of your father. Tomorrow my soul will pass away through the chimney that smokes day and night. Come and I shall bless you before my death, you, my youngest son, Yaakov: "May Jehovah answer you in your days of distress. May the name of the God of Jacob protect you. The angel that did not succeed in redeeming me in time from the claws of the Nazi soldiers - may their name and memory be forever obliterated - may he redeem you and guard you from all evil; and when you succeed, privileged by luck to get through this Shoah, remember lest you forget, the things that your eyes have seen, and teach them scrupulously to your children, your grandchildren, your great grandchildren, and to all the generations that come after you, and you shall talk of them when you sit at home and when you walk along the road, when you lay down to sleep and when you get up."

His blessing was fulfilled! Like the pillar of fire that illuminated the desert for the children of Israel when they left Egypt, the blessing turned darkness into light and saved me from the claws of death all the years of the Shoah. The last remnant was not obliterated. From his three sons, I was the only one left, and then I swore: "May my right hand forget its skill, may my tongue cling to the roof of my mouth, if I shall not consider those who perished, at the times of my greatest joy."

My brother Yehudah also reached Majdanek at this time, but we entered the camp separately. He entered the extermination camp in the same manner as I did. He took leave of father and got his blessing too.

My deceased father, who went as a sacrifice to the Moloch in Majdanek, he whose house was a meeting place for the Jewish community elders, he who was a pursuer of peace, he who loved mankind, he who fulfilled the "mitzvahs" [commandments] not in order to get a reward... his ashes were scattered and "fertilised" the fields of Poland.

A Song with No Name

[Translated from the original in Polish, which is in rhyme]

And when the cruel enemy crossed
The golden threshold of our homeland
The sun hid itself beyond the clouds
The day became sad and gloomy

Abandon your family nest
Wander in other directions
So commanded the enemy for its convenience;
With no fear ofpunishment from God

I part from you the fields, the forests and the rivers
The very beautiful and beloved farms of my homeland
Goodbye to thehouses and to my home town
In which I spent the years of my childhood

I take leave of you my beloved garden
And the beautiful orchard situated by the waters
Where the storks settled on the poplar trees
And the bees crowded together in the fields

When one looks at everything
With pain in our hearts, wiping away a tear with a handkerchief

Oh God take pity on us; why have you punished us like this?
You stole these treasures from our forefathers

Where are you, our dear and beloved father and mother?
You died of hunger in unknown places
Our sisters were sent to another country to work
Our brother was taken to the slaughter by the Ukrainians

Where are you my beloved bride?
The only coddled daughter of her mother?
Your body riddled in bullets.
Christ! Is any greater pain than this possible?

All of you rest in dark graves
I shall no longer have any pleasant moments
Whenever I remem-ber these things
But I shall never forget you

The cold snow covers your graves
In autumn the sad rain will cover you
In spring the lark will sing for you
In summer a nightingale will sadden you with its song

On the cross a lost crow will call out
And a tired passer-by will cry and say a prayer
Guard us God from sudden death by a Ukrainian knife
That death of hunger may never return

However, you did not [hear our cry]
Despite your people [who were suffering and rotting]
The best of your sons were sent to the gallows
How terrible is the bloodshed

In the camps children are asking for a drop of milk
The old are awaiting a slice of bread and are dying of hunger
Our ǎvant-garde" is carrying the burden of slavery
"Sursum Corda" [lift up your hearts] in this tragedy

And when judgement day arrives
The walls will come down and the grates will break open You
shall stand tall Poland and shake yourself free of your
shackles Your crying will turn into dance

J. Ciszewski 5 July 1943

The Wandering Period

After the departure of the Germans from the district, bands of Poles and Ukrainians started to fight with each other in order to gain control of the villages. I didn't join these battles and then the suspicions of the Poles that I was a Jew grew even stronger.

One day a guest, who was a Christian from my home town Skulsk, came to the Paritz's Manor House. He was looking for work in the area and the Paritz accepted him for work on his estate. As on any other evening, at the end of the working day we all sat down to dinner in the kitchen at the Paritz's house. The guy identified me immediately and then he asked me directly if I was Yaakov Kotowski, a Jew from Skulsk. I laughed and told him that that was impossible and that of course I was not a Jew. But, my blood froze in my veins and I was gripped by fear.

The Polish partisans understood that all their suspicions about me were not unfounded, and because they were driven senseless by their anti-Semitism, even my best friends among them preferred to see me dead once they discovered that I was a Jew; and indeed, one of them went and informed on me to the Gestapo. He told them that I was a Jew and that I was the one who had spied for them during the time of the battles. When the Gestapo heard that I was the spy, obviously they came out immediately and tried to catch me.

The penny dropped and I understood that the arrival of this

gentile at the estate constituted a real danger for me, so I decided to run away that very night. Without informing the Paritz or anybody else on the farm I fled to Husynne, the village where my brother Yehudah lived. I settled on the other side of the village so that no one would make any connection between us. I started to work for a living at the new Paritz's estate, as Head Gardner.

For a while everything was fine. But as destiny would have it, a Polish "bastard" who knew me from Cichoborz came to this village. The Ukrainians burnt down the village where he had lived so he came to Husynne and lived at his uncle's. He recognised me and immediately went to the Gestapo to inform on me that I was a Jew. When the Gestapo heard this, they came out immediately to look for me.

It was in the middle of a wintery night. One of my friends came running at the last minute, to let me know that somebody had informed on me to the Gestapo and that they were on my tracks and were coming to get me. I jumped out of the window wearing only the robe that was on my body and disappeared.

Outside it was bitterly cold and complete darkness. I escaped without knowing where my legs were carrying me. I could already hear the dogs barking from far away, and I understood that the Germans were chasing after me.

I ran with all my might without knowing the way, and suddenly I saw a house. I decided to try and go inside it. In this house lived a Christian woman and her only daughter. I knocked at the door and the woman opened it for me. I told her that the Germans are chasing me and I begged her to hide me. The Christian woman and her daughter crossed themselves and I could see that they were hesitating and didn't know what to do. They knew that if they handed me over to the Germans I would meet with a bitter end and on the other hand, they knew that if I was caught hiding in their house, their end would be bitter too. In the end they let me in and found a hiding place for me.

In Poland it is very cold in winter and people have big stoves at home. In their house the stove was wide and its height almost reached the ceiling. There was a narrow gap between the stove and the wall and they hid me there. The stove was burning, the heat was unbearable and there wasn't enough air.

Suddenly a strong knock on the door was heard that was accompanied by shouting to open up immediately. The frightened woman and her daughter opened the door and the Germans entered the house to look for me. The Germans asked if anybody entered the house and they said no. The Germans didn't believe them and started to search for me all over the house. I stopped breathing out of fear; my entire body was burning from the heat of the stove. I saw the mother and daughter through a crack; they crossed themselves again and again and mumbled a prayer.

It didn't occur to the Germans to look for me behind the stove and after a while they left the house. A miracle had occurred; I managed to escape the clutches of their murderous claws, moments before certain death.

Burnt from the heat, after having almost suffocated, they pulled me out, half unconscious. Slowly I began to recover and begged that they let me stay for the night in their house. I assumed that the Germans would not come back to the same house to look for me again, in addition to which I had no place else to go on such a cold night. I promised that I would leave early the following morning, they agreed and I did indeed leave the following day.

On that day: "A shoot will come out from the stump of Jesse [Yishai]; from his roots a branch will bear fruit, that will not continue to rely on the one who beat him anymore. Has the lord struck her as he struck down those who struck her? Has she been killed as those were killed who killed her? You will tread on the lion and the cobra; you will trample the great lion and the serpent, and you broke the teeth of the wicked".

What I want to say is that after all of this, I started to think differently. I asked myself: How many sacrifices were offered up to foreign alters by the Jews in the killing fields? How many rivers of blood flowed and mountains of ashes piled up by us? And what did we get in return? We were ridiculed and made a mockery of, as sheep led to the slaughter, and we having sacrificed so much to the Moloch. How many times had I risked my life? I fought as a soldier in the Polish army; I was a spy for the Polish partisans, and what was to be my reward in return? The same Poles I had helped informed on me to the Germans telling them that I was a Jew and that I was the spy. Consequently, from that point on, I decided that I would no longer join forces with the Polish partisans but that I would only look out for myself and do all that I could to save my own life, from then on, I just wanted to live in peace until the end of the war.

After the Germans discovered that I was the spy and knew that I was no longer around, they didn't fear coming back to Cichoborz and its countryside. They took control of the area again and went back to taking all of the agricultural produce for their own needs.

The Germans started to search for me, and all over the area of the River Wisla and the Bug there were posters proclaiming that whoever found me, came across my tracks, informed on me or brought substantial information about me, would be given a reward of the considerable sum of 45,000 Rentenmarks; in those days this was a dream-like sum of money.

I was tormented by my own thoughts: What would happen to me now? Where could I turn? Where would I go? The Germans were on my tracks and my picture could be found in every corner; my life was in great danger, where could I hide from them? That was when I escaped to the only place where I could find shelter; I ran to the forest. In the rain, in the snow, hungry and in the cold, the forest became my temporary home.

I lived in the county of Hrubieszow on the Bug's riverbank, but in every town or village I wandered into I saw my picture, as a wanted man; therefore, I had to keep moving all the time. During my wanderings my beard grew long, my hair grew wild, I grew a Polish moustache and I looked like a "prehistoric man"; my clothes were worn out and torn and sometimes I was unable to wash for a long time. I walked using a stick, all my property was the sack I carried on my back, I became a vagabond.

Since I had been informed on and my name was known I had to get a new identity card. During my wanderings I met a railway worker who had escaped from Kowel. We met by accident, and he told me that he was going to travel to visit his family the following morning. He left his coat hanging on a tree stump overnight. I took his identity card out of his wallet and made a run for it. From that moment on I had a new identity. I turned from Ciszewski Jan to Kubicki Grzegorz. However, his year of birth was 1882 and mine was 1911; almost thirty years difference. I had to correct the identity card. This time there was nobody who could do it for me professionally; therefore, I changed the two middle numbers myself and turned the year of birth into 1912. From that moment that was it! There was no more Ciszewski Jan; from that day on I was Kubicki Grzegorz. And again; "and they travelled…and they camped"; I continued on my wanderings.

I wandered on; wanting to reach another village in order to look for work, but the Germans had checkpoints on the roads that were located at the entrance to every village. At these checkpoints they would check the documents of whoever passed through. I reached a place where I had no choice but to pass through such a checkpoint in order to progress. The clerk who sat at the checkpoint took my papers for examination and saw that there was a correction to the original year of birth. He showed it to his commander and after a short investigation the latter ordered they put me in a detention cell immediately. They decided that they would hang me the following morning. Death was staring me in the face and my life flashed before my eyes, I understood that my life was coming to an end and I prepared myself for death.

I don't know how, it was my good fortune, but that night, the Gestapo's station commander returned to the camp in his vehicle; he was as drunk as Lot, joyful, happy and good hearted, singing and dancing, swaying from side to side like a Lulav, and then he gave his clerk the order: "Release him". The clerk couldn't believe it and hesitated. Then the commander shouted at him in a loud voice: "Release him!" and release me he did, in spite of his reservations.

I, who had already prepared myself for death, left the detention cell and after distancing myself from the place, ran with all my might, until eventually I sat down on a rock in the middle of nowhere. I pinched myself again and again, checking to see whether this was a dream or reality? My heart pounded strongly and then I understood, once again my life had been hanging by a thread, a great miracle had occurred and I was saved.

I wandered from place to place looking for work. Once again, I was forced to change my identity and this time too there was no one who could do it for me professionally, so I took a simple pen and I changed the documents myself. I changed only one letter in the documents, so that the change would be minute and I went on my way. I changed my name from Kubicki Grzegorz to Kubacki Grzegorz. The canvass is too short to describe everything I went through; somehow, by luck alone I survived. Ultimately, I changed my name three times over the course of the war.

Before the war we used to trade with the Polish Paritzs. Among these Paritzs was the Tabaczynski family, who were considered to be Polish nobility. The Paritz Jan Tabaczynski and his family were from the village Raciecin, which was not far from Skulsk.He used to come to buy building materials from us and liked to stay for dinner at our house, since mother prepared Gefilte Fish that was to his liking. The connection between our families had started from the time of his grandfather and father, who had also traded with us. As children we grew up together.

During the war the Germans divided Poland into two parts: one part, where only Germans lived, was annexed to the German Reich, and the other part was defined as "Mandatory Poland" and was under German occupation; this was where the Polish population and nobility were deported to. The Germans killed some of the Polish Paritzs and some of the others who survived were dispersed over different villages in Mandatory Poland. The Paritz Jan Tabaczynski was also deported to one of these remote villages, called Rzadca.

It was a cold rainy day, towards nightfall darkness prevailed and everything turned pitch black. I wandered to the edge of one of the villages and tried my luck. Maybe I would succeed in getting into one of the houses. I was very hungry and I also hoped that maybe I would finally manage to spend the night inside one of the houses, after a long period in which I had only slept outdoors. To my surprise I saw the figure of Paritz Jan Tabaczynski in the courtyard of one of the houses.

I approached and knocked on the door of his house. I was met by his wife. I stood up straight, my teeth chattering and my body shivering, as I was completely wet. I recognised the Paritz's wife immediately; I kissed her hand and asked for something to eat. "Jesus Maria" she said "Who are you and what do you want?" I told her that I was from Skulsk. "What did you do there?" she asked, and I replied: "My father was a poor tailor and cobbler." "And what is your name?" I said that my name was Kubacki Grzegorz and she responded that she didn't know me. "Since you are from Skulsk you are welcome to come in" she said, and she gave me some food. After that she called her son and said: "Call your father and tell him that we have got a visitor from Skulsk, surely he will be very happy."

Five minutes passed before Paritz Tabaczynski arrived. I recognised him from the moment that I saw him in the court-yard. Now he stood in front of me in all his grandeur. He entered the dining room and saw me, but he did not recognise me. He got a fright when he saw me because I looked like a savage. Then he started to converse with me and asked me "Where are you from?" and I replied: "I am from Skulsk and I think that you are the Paritz Tabaczynski and that your estate is in Raciecin; anybody from Skulsk knows you, an honourable gentleman." "What are you doing here? What do you want you poor thing?" And I replied: "My father was a poor tailor and cobbler in Skulsk. The Germans deported us and I arrived here by chance. I am looking for work. Maybe you will take pity on me and employ me?" And he replied: "Certainly, certainly I will help a poor man like you, especially since you are from my home town. Tomorrow I shall give you work as a gardener, but first let's sit and have supper for now. You will lodge at my house and tomorrow morning I shall give you new clothes and some money so that you can get a haircut, then you will go to the head of the village to register as my employee and you will work for me until the end of the war." In that moment I thought to myself that I was in great luck and that nothing could be better than this.

We ate and drank to our heart's content, like kings. Around the table also sat a woman I didn't know, with her child. Without warning an unexpected question suddenly came up: "Did you know the Jews of Skulsk? Can you tell me what became of them?

Surely you knew Itcze and Gitel Kotowski, Aharon, Yehudah and Yaakov Kotowski." I felt fear and trepidation. For a moment I recalled my home; we were all there together, a loving and united family; what beautiful days we had experienced together. I regained my composure, I put on the face of a typical Jew hater, and then I answered him with restraint: "Why are you asking me about those damned leper Jews. You would do better to ask me about our poor Poles who are dropping like flies for our dear homeland; the Germans are shooting them to death every day. But he went on: "Did you hear what destiny befell Itcze Kotowski?" and I answered: "Yes, I knew him, but they are all gone." And he continued: "You did not know those Jews like I did; it is a shame about them, they were good Jews." I reacted to these things and answered: "Yes, I have heard of them, but the Germans have already killed them all to the best of my knowledge." In that moment Tabaczynski sounded desperately nostalgic and his curiosity got the better of him, taking him over like a dybbuk. He continued to ask me questions, about the Nasielski family, who were among our close acquaintances, and about the family of Halina Radiczewski. Halina was a relative of ours and her family was as rich as the Tabaczynski family. They were estates owners with large farms and they employed many workers, they also had diverse trading relationships. I was very agitated by this entire conversation.

On the following morning I went to register with the head of the village. When the head of the village saw my identity card, he immediately suspected that I was a Jew. He went out to bridle his horses with the intention of going to the Gestapo in the county capital in order to inform on me to them. I do not know how I managed to deceive him and convince him that he was wrong. Again, it was only by some miracle that I managed to slip out of his grip, otherwise today you would have found me on the holy steps, as one of the foot-rests under the heavenly throne. Whilst fleeing from him I saw "wanted" posters for Jan Ciszewski in every corner. I left for Winiory, not far from Sandomierz. I arrived at the new village and went into an estate there. The hour was late and I saw the old wife of the "Paritz" sitting down with the young "Shikse'lech" [non-Jewish maids]. They were singing the Polish song "Majowe Nieszporg" ["Psalms of the month of May"]. I kneeled and sang together with them till the end of the song.

"What do you want?" asked me the old wife of the "Paritz". "I ran away from Kowel from the Russian's Katyusha rockets. They destroyed everything and killed everybody. I was the only one left and I don't have what to live off." "Come into the kitchen; I will get you something to eat. The master will return later and he will surely give you some work. We have a lot of refugees from Kowel here." I quickly made friends with everybody there.

The master arrived towards evening and called me to him: "I heard your story and tomorrow I will definitely get you some work. We Polish brothers should surely help each other in such bitter times. We can hear the sound of the Russian artillery over the horizon, and liberation is near. Give me your identity card, tomorrow I am going to Sandomierz and I will register you."

I gave him my identity card and he studied it for a second. Suddenly his facial expression became strange. He raised his eyes from the identity card and examined me thoroughly; he looked me over from top to bottom and immediately said: "Pannie Kochany" [dear friend], run away as fast as you can from this area. Do not register anywhere in these surroundings, because all around the area of Sandomierz there are "wanted" posters of you: "A Jew with Aryan Papers", "The Spy From Hrubieszow", "Secret Agent of the Partisans at the Gestapo", "Schtinker" [informer], "Rat for the Polish Partisans". You also stole an identity card from the railway worker Kubicki Grzegorz. A reward of 45,000 Rentenmarks has been offered for your whereabouts. You got lucky with me; I shall give you some clothes and some money, but be on your way. Go far away from here towards the Wisla." Once again, a miracle occurred to me on the banks of the river Bug.

Once again, I wandered about, heading towards the Wisla. This time I reached Jaworzno, adjacent to the town of Czestochowa, and there I went to Sir Jaza to look for work. He agreed that I could work in his house, but first I had to go and register with the commander of the Gestapo, Mr. Schulz. He was a cruel and dangerous murderer that would not let a cat or a dog pass four feet from him without shooting it. The kind of person who has a terrible reputation-his murderous name was the fear of every leaving soul, all over the Czestochowa County in the south west of Poland.

I didn't have any choice but to enter the office of this violent Gestapo officer. On his table lay a Browning pistol and if that was not enough, next to it a Mauser rifle as well. How it was that I didn't run away from there immediately defies all logic, since I was convinced that I would not make it out of there alive.

He looked at my forged identity card with the corrections and growled at me: "You can wipe your ass with this document." I was in shock for a moment; I did not know how to respond. I felt that the end was coming. I do not know what gave me the idea, but at that moment it came to me; "Sir Commander; I came here from Kowel. A heavy bombardment took place there and we had to evacuate the place within an hour. I couldn't find my identity card and I had to get a new one issued. The clerk prepared it for me in haste; he made a mistake and then corrected it." Schulz thought for a moment and then said: "That is possible, you are right." And once again a miracle took place, maybe by the grace of the Black Madonna from Czestochowa, the famous icon of The Mother of God that made Czestochowa sacred to the observant Christians Poles.

After some time, I was forced to go on in my wanderings again. I reached Jedrzejow; there I went to Mr. Sobczyk, who was formerly a Member of Parliament in the county of Kielce, and from then on I worked for him.

184 | SCATTERED RAYS OF LIGHT

Germany

Hanna: Ida and Anton worked in Dresden. Anton worked in an arms factory and Ida in a restaurant, every day at lunchtime she served a hot meal and at five o'clock in the afternoon she would serve coffee and cakes to people who came off the street to eat in the restaurant.

I waited impatiently for an answer from them. Days passed and the situation in the estate started to become more difficult. At nights the Polish partisans would come and take everything that Yaakov had produced from the milk, since the Germans had lost control of the place.

After three weeks I received a document from Dresden that said that I was needed to work in a restaurant. On the envelope there were stamps displaying the swastika and the letter was signed by the German police.

I started to prepare for travel. My landlady was prepared to give me anything if only I would stay; she knew only too well that she wouldn't find someone like me to help her. I told her that I had no more contact with Janusz and that consequently I wanted to leave. Not long after, I left.

From Cichoborz I arrived by train in Lublin, there was a big camp there where all the Polish youth had gathered. The camp was full of Poles, Ukrainians and common Germans. There I felt Polish and had no reason to fear anything, at least so it seemed to me at first. I waited for two days to be sent to Germany; but I was mistaken...

In the camp there were three managers who were in charge of transferring people to work in Germany. I had the papers and I knew where I was to be sent, that's why I was sure that everything would turn out alright. One day they called me to the office and told me that I was a Jewess and that I wanted to go to Germany because that was customary in Poland. I said that of course I wasn't a Jewess and that I had no connection with the Jews. They threw me into a holding room and tortured me for a couple of hours. In my imagination I could see my mother, may she R.I.P., there next to me, telling me to say: "No, no!" That night they took me again in order to torture me some more, but there was another Polish girl in the room called Hanka Szosda, who knew me from Cichoborz, and she said to them: "Are you mad? I know Hanka and I categorically assure you that she is Polish." With these words she simply brought me back to life.

I was not sent to the destination in accordance with the papers that I held. Forty young people, among them Hanka Szosda and myself, were sent towards the Dutch border to work in a knitwear factory. There, I became the leader of the young women who worked there since I spoke a bit of German.

We resided in a big hotel in the city of Kempen-Krefeld. The work wasn't bad, but I wanted to be together with Ida and Anton, therefore every day I would go to the offices to ask them to let me go to Dresden. During all this period I had contact with Ida and Anton by correspondence and they were waiting for me.

In this way three months went by and eventually they gave me money and told me to go any which way. When they told me that I could go, I asked one of the young women who worked with me in the knitwear factory to buy me the ticket to Dresden. I was afraid to buy the ticket myself since all the stations in the town of Kempen were full of German army and police people. Germany was still in the middle of a war. The young woman bought me the ticket; I took my leave from Hanka and travelled to Dresden that night.

On the train there were only soldiers. I was the only woman among the passengers. I sat all night on a bench without talking to anyone. I travelled like this for twelve hours and reached Dresden in the morning.

I had the address of Ida and Anton but I didn't know how to get to them.

During the time that I worked in the knitwear factory I spoke and learnt a bit more German. I approached an old man and asked him in German where Wilder street was. The man helped me carry my suitcase. I followed him to the trolleybus station which brought me to Ida's house.

At that time Ida was at work and Anton, her husband, was in the factory. There are no words to describe the moment when we met and the joy of being together.

I started to work in the same restaurant as Ida worked. The restaurant owner and her sister received me warmly, in spite of the fact that the restaurant owner's husband had passed away at the time. We all lived in the same building where the restaurant was located, Ida and Anton on one floor, and I, on my own, on another floor.

A German couple with whom we had good relations lived on the same street. They had three daughters and one son. The son was fighting on the Russian border and he came home to visit his parents from time to time. One evening we were at home and the mother came to visit us. She laughed profusely and said that her son, Adel, had said that I Hanna was a Jewess and that I looked just like those Jews who obtained forged papers. We were very scared that he would come to us, and we didn't go to visit them anymore. At a later stage the parents were notified that the Russians had killed their son.

We lived in fear that someone would identify us the entire time. Anton was also very afraid to work in the factory, when he returned home from work, he used to put beer on his hair to smooth it down.

We lived in this situation for two years, always in the hope that the war would finally end. One evening, the restaurant's owner came to our room and gave us some bad news. She said that she had been ordered by the Gestapo and the high officers to close the restaurant. Instead of the restaurant a station to treat wounded army personnel who returned from the borders would be established there; this meant that all the current workers would be fired since they had their own people. It was a dark night for us, we understood that we would have to move and live with the Polish workers, in their sheds, from where they would send us to work in the war.

For a few days we walked around completely desperate, we didn't know what to do, Anton and Ida cried. One day I looked downstairs and saw a group of the Gestapo's people chatting to each other. I went downstairs and with my basic German I implored them to take us to work for them, saying that we were ready to do any work, even to peel potatoes, just as long as we wouldn't have to go and live with the workers from all over the world who lived in sheds.

All those who had previously worked in the restaurant were not accepted for work, but they must have taken pity on us since they let us stay and work in the "Lazarett" [The hospital in Dresden]. Ida and I worked very hard for about six months, over time they saw that we were quiet and didn't make any trouble, so they gave us better work to do.

Below are the details of Hanna's German work permit:

Work Permit

Family name: Kotecka   First name: Anna Date of Birth: 2 July 1922
Place of birth: Cichoborz   District: Hrubieszow Citizenship:
Without citizenship (Polish)
Profession and professional group: Kitchen assistant 22 a 1 Registry
Number: EK. 179/362

Employer: Reserve Lazarett Dresden 7
Work place address: Dresden N.23, RTsaer Place 22   District:
Dresden
Registered on: 3 July1943   Valid till: 31 January 1945

One Sunday morning, to our great surprise, Shulem Frenkel, a child-hood friend of ours from school arrived. I had had the intention of marrying Shulem back at the time when we lived in Skulsk, but the war had separated us. During the time of the war he had started going out with another woman called Marta. Marta was a woman who had worked for us at our house in Skulsk. We were all very scared; Anton thought that he was going to have a heart attack. We were afraid that someone would see them in our room, so we asked them to take pity on us, leave, and not return again.

Shulem and Marta moved to a private house, and Marta was scared that Shulem would want to be my boyfriend again. One day I went to visit them. Marta had a big and dirty mouth and she said to me: "Next time you come I shall go and inform on you to the Gestapo, now I am with Shulem and you don't have any business here." I didn't go to visit them again.

During that period, our life was relatively good. We had many foreign acquaintances; from Belgium, Czechia and also some French captives from Algeria. Many Germans wanted to go out with me because I was a young woman, and they would say to me: "We know that you are Polish, but you are different, that's why we want to go out with you". I didn't want to be with them so I befriended one of the French Algerians who worked with me in the hospital, his name was Roland Huillet, and we spent a lot of time together. We went to the theatre and the cinema together, and on our free days we would go dancing in one of the coffee shops.

Dresden was a beautiful city. All the big buildings were built in the Baroque style. The trolleybus stopped at "Zwinger" and at "Wissen

Hissel". These coffee shops stood out because of their beauty and architectural poles. I took advantage of all the good things that the city could bestow on me.

I started to work in the hospital at night, as the person who listened to the radio in order to alert every one of the sirens, since there were many bombardments of Germany at the time. There was a big radio here, from which the wounded German soldiers could also hear the sirens while they were in their beds. One night Roland changed the radio wave to the BBC's broadcast channel and he forgot to close the lines by which the broadcast was also transferred to the patients' rooms, and everyone heard the news from England. The moment this was discovered I thought was going to be our end. I asked Roland to go and I settled the matter with the officer who was in charge of the department.

We heard what was going on in other countries and we knew what was happening on the borders. At night Ida and I often prepared hot wine for the soldiers who were brought in from the Russian border.

Anton Piotrowski

Ida Piotrowski

Auschwitz-Birkenau

Carla: We were sent to Auschwitz. They put us onto train carriages in unspeakable conditions. We had to lie one on top of another, men and women together, and it was very easy to suffocate. That was when we began to understand what was in store for us. We, the Jews of Holland, were not used to such difficult conditions. The status of the Jews in Holland had been much higher than that of the Jews in Poland, and also than that of Jews in other places. We couldn't imagine that we, citizens with equal rights, would be expelled from Holland. Therefore the shock was immense.

I can't remember how long that journey of torment, in those over packed freight wagons was, we felt like it lasted an eternity. It is impossible to describe the journey, the scenes which we witnessed inside the wagons were tragic; fear, anxiety, filth, there wasn't any water and there wasn't any air. We were transported like cattle.

Eventually we reached Auschwitz. I didn't know where I was or what Auschwitz was. It is hard to describe in words our first minutes on that notorious platform in Auschwitz. The moment we set foot off the carriages our "reception" was to be beaten. They shouted and beat us; I saw how they took my neighbour's child with my own eyes, how they tore children from their mothers' arms and how they threw toddlers by their hands and feet against a wall. It was a horrible scene that cannot be described in words; one that was burned into the eyes of anyone who saw it, and can never be forgotten, real hell. They started the "selection", men to one side and women to the other. They took whatever we had on us by force. We were then led into the "Lager" [the camp], where the dogs attacked us, bit us and left us bleeding. Inside the camp we were divided up and led into sheds, the condition of the sheds was awful.

The following morning,I looked outside and I saw hundreds, thousands, of women and men with shaved heads, in worn out clothing, and they all looked starved. They signalled to us that they were hungry and indicated that they wanted us to throw them some food. I asked myself, how could anyone live like this? How could a human being prevail under these conditions? Indeed, it was like a mad house... I still thought that they didn't mean to do the same to us...that they wouldn't leave us, the Jews of Holland, here, that they would take us somewhere else. God, where were we? ...

The moment that we reached Auschwitz, I threw all the valuables that were sewn into my clothes into the latrines so that the Germans would not benefit in any way from them.

Half an hour later some Ukrainians entered our shed, they abused us, dragged us to "the sauna", for that was what they called it, and there they were even more brutal. They tore our clothes from us, made us stand on a chair, shaved off our hair and searched the intimate parts of our bodies to make sure we weren't hiding anything. They were looking for gold, diamonds, money, foreign currency, dollars. They searched inside our body cavities using their fingers. I felt sick, but I was helpless, we were in their hands and became their property. We were washed with cold water and after that with hot water, and our clothes were taken from us. We were given the clothes of Russian prisoners of war, filthy uniforms full of lice. It was truly horrific. The names of the prisoners of war were displayed on the uniforms, Lieutenant so and so etc. Thus our tragedy began.

I arrived at Auschwitz in the middle of July 1942; I can't remember the exact date. It was hot; it was in the middle of the summer. We slept on straw mattresses that were also full of lice. The lice literally ate us; they bit us and sucked our blood. The mattresses cut our flesh. In addition, we were forced to go out to work in the fields, exposed and without any shoes; if we somehow got hold of any shoes, we were not allowed to wear them, we had to carry them on our shoulders. The "Capos" took care of that; this was how they began our torment in Auschwitz.

After a few days they numbered us; they tattooed a number on the arm of each of us, my number was: 8846.

After a short while, we were told that all the Dutch citizens must report to them separately.I believed that we would be sent to a more comfortable place. How naïve could I be? For when a person is in the depth of despair, he clings to any glimmer of hope... But the enormity of the disaster only became clear when we realized that we had been transferred to Birkenau. There the severity of the tragedy was even greater than in Auschwitz. There all hope was lost and we could visualise our imminent demise. Even now, as I recount this, I wonder how one can even begin to describe the monstrosity, the human catastrophe, of the extermination machine, devised, instigated and operated by the Germans at such a pace.

In Birkenau there were no dormitory blocks in the beginning. There was no place to lie down at all. The flies, the lice and the mice abused our bodies. Rats as big as dogs bit us, it was terrible. We were led to work with dogs.

Gradually we started to get used to this hell. This proves that a human being can suffer anything. For a long time, I couldn't taste the bread that we received. For whole days I didn't ask for bread since I felt so awful, but I did not give up, I didn't lose the courage in my heart nor what was left of my strength. I was more optimistic than all the others who were around me. I told myself that I mustn't become apathetic and that I had to resist with all my strength so as not to lose the will to live, since that would be the end of me; I knew that if I didn't take care of myself, death would be unavoidable, that if I didn't grow stronger my fate would be the same as that of many others.

Additional transports arrived from Holland. Native Dutch people were unable to face the horror, and by the second day of their time at Auschwitz they ran into the electric wire fences, were they were electrocuted and relieved of all their troubles. They were looking for a way to end it all, and this was it. By the third day they had already reached the crematorium. But there were people who said to me, Carla, resist, tomorrow we will be released. This was the Dutch optimism I thought to myself…

We, the Polish Jews, were familiar with the surroundings and the language. When we were approached in Dutch we could also understand. In this respect our situation in hell was better than that of the native Dutch Jews, who other than their own language didn't speak any Slav languages. Even when we were approached in German or Czech we understood. When the Capos said "Right!" they walked to the left and when they said "Left!" they walked to the right, everything was the wrong way around.

I was forced to do exhausting types of labour, digging and carrying rocks. The work was not productive; it was just to exhaust us, to keep us busy doing very tiring tasks, this was their system. We destroyed buildings and then reconstructed them, destroyed them again and rebuilt them. Like Sisyphus, we carried rocks the whole time. I don't know where I drew the strength to work so hard, under such terrible conditions, without the necessary calories, without decent food and without rest. This is how it was, in the summer in terrible heat, and in the winter in the snow and in the bitter cold; my feet literally froze from the snow; after the war two of my toes had to be amputated surgically, one from each foot.

Every day we received a piece of bread, a small slice with a bit of margarine on it and some tea. It was impossible to drink the tea, it was nauseatingly bitter, and by the time we got any of this we had almost perished. Anyone who hasn't experienced this themselves will never be able to understand. I am unable to understand how I prevailed.

We lay down to sleep on wooden boards that were horribly crowded; five, six women together, sometimes it reached even ten - women from France, Poland and Slovakia. Nobody spoke about taking a shower or washing; during the three years that I was at Birkenau I never washed properly, not even once. The lice bit me, I was filthy, and all my body was covered in sores from top to bottom. I had two deep lesions on my face, from the lice and the dirt.

I walked out first to every selection, what would be, would be. I couldn't find a worse hell than this one. Before each selection I would pinch my cheeks so that they would seem to have some colour in them, and so that I would give a better impression. I don't know how I survived all those selections. I always saw Doctor Mengele standing before me and it was as if I was seeing the angel of death; I carry his picture in my wallet, in case he is ever caught; I shall be the first to testify against him. I had time to get to know him "only too well"; even if he has changed his facial features or even if he has had plastic surgery, I will recognise him. But regrettably in the meantime he is still walking free…

As I already said, the conditions of our existence, if one can even call this "existence or life", were characterised by "sub- human conditions". The mortality rate was acute; human beings were dropping like flies. Words lost all value and meaning; we became a number, no more. Birkenau was the embodiment of hell. The frequent selections come up before my eyes over and over again. I also see how they used to pull and drag out the sick people from the wooden boards, taking the weakest people. Vehicles would drive up and the sick would be thrown into them as if they were stones, and they were then led to block number 8; the block that was destined for those who were condemned to die and who would then be transported to the crematoriums. On one occasion I myself was led to block number 8. I was very weak and indifferent; I didn't have the energy to resist, I was just waiting for the moment when all my torments would come to an end. I was fed up of my life, how long could one endure?

I too was among those that they threw into a vehicle and transferred to the gas chambers, later headed for the crematoriums. I was probably so helpless that I didn't react at all to everything that was happening around me, with complete acceptance of my fate. I stood in the line of people at the entrance to the gas chambers and I was unable to explain to myself where I was standing. For a moment my mind became clear and I grasped that now it really was the end, the end of suffering. I was sick then, with scarlet fever, and I was running a high fever. While I was standing in line, a few paces before the entrance, lost and unable to do anything, a German passed by and in his attempt to push through us, he gave me a horrible blow with his fist. I fell to the ground on the spot, and that was where I remained, stretched out on the ground, as if dead...

Night had fallen. All of the others had been taken into the gas chambers and I was still lying on the ground in the dark. At some point I regained my senses and succeeded in organising my thoughts. It was winter, it was really freezing outside, I rubbed snow all over my face and got up slowly, and then I cautiously started to crawl towards my block. On my way there I wondered: Had one of the Germans perhaps taken down my number? Indeed,it was impossible that the Germans,with their systematic meticulousness and order, would forget to do so. Maybe they would calculate exactly how many people were burnt in the crematorium that day and would discover that one prisoner was missing? I was horribly scared that they would look for me in the block, find me and take me back to suffocate in the gas chambers. A friend of mine said to me: "Carla, don't worry", but I was scared that at any moment they would call out my name. Indeed;

I had been condemned to death, I had already been at the entrance to the gas chamber...

In this way, I evaded death time after time. How come? I do not know myself. But that event, the blow I was given by the German when I was at the entrance to the gas chambers that saved me from death, is engraved in my memory. Even today I cannot understand how I stayed alive, how they didn't see me lying at the entrance to the gas chamber and didn't just drag me inside too.

This incident brought me to the decision that I should not commit suicide. Many times I watched how my girlfriends succumbed to the worst of all and threw themselves against the electric wire fences. But I decided, I would not go to the electric fence. If I had been saved from the gas chamber, I must stay alive and not electrocute myself; I would stay alive at all costs. As far as it depended on me alone, I would not commit suicide.

Some men came to work in our block. While they worked, they asked me where I was from. I told them that I was from Holland and that my husband was David Lewenoff from Amsterdam. Immediately somebody said that he knew him and that he was working in block number 18. There was no end to my happiness. I asked them to send him my regards and later I received a short letter from him. I also succeeded in transferring a small note to him. I covered it in snow and made a snow ball, which I then threw towards him. If the Germans had noticed this, I would have received a fatal punishment.

In time, I recovered and I felt stronger than my friends. I took care to save my strength despite not getting extra portions of food. My husband was a weak man physically; therefore I decided to help him. I saved some of my bread and food and passed it on to him in a variety of ways whenever I could.

Every day at four o'clock in the morning there was an "Appel" [roll call], it was awful. They gathered everybody in the head count field, without any food or water, and there your destiny was determined.

We were condemned to die at any given moment. In summer it was in the heat, and in winter it was in the freezing cold. They kept us in that field for hours. Every minute we were condemned to death. Who can describe the beatings that we received? After the head count we were sent to work. In order not to be seen as weak or sickly in the eyes of the Germans I was very careful about one thing; never to walk bent over; I always tried to walk upright.

I kept myself from being beaten; for example, at the time of food distribution, unlike many others, I didn't attack, since those who pushed were beaten and often they ended up first in line for the selection. When everybody pushed to get bread and potatoes, I moved away. One woman, who was in charge of one of the blocks noticed this and probably appreciated it. Her name was Eta Gutman, she was a Jew from Czechoslovakia, I have to say that I owe her a great deal. Over time she tried to help me, and she would always pass me a slice of bread. Only someone who knows what the meaning of a slice of bread in Birkenau was is able to understand and appreciate the meaning of this.

One day my husband and I set up a meeting. I told the woman who was responsible for my block about it. She gave me an item of clothing that looked a bit better than mine for the meeting and said: "Carla, you are going to meet your husband, take this piece of clothing, at least you will look a bit more human." She also gave me a small slice of bread; really, she pushed it into my hand.

The meeting had to be in the small room where he worked; my husband worked in the "commando". The woman who was responsible for my block agreed with the woman who was in charge of the "commando" that she would turn a blind eye at the time of the meeting with my husband (they had a good relationship).

The man who guarded the men happened to be Dutch, and in a moment of weakness he had told my husband that he was German by origin, a soldier that was transferred to Holland, that he was not a devotee of Hitler and that he hated the Nazis. He said to my husband: "If the subject of your "discussion" is really your wife, go to the meeting."

And indeed, in this way my husband and I managed to meet in the horrible death camp. It was an emotional meeting, both of us in a "Lager", both of us condemned to death, who knew if we would survive...

But the meeting later caused me great suffering, a fact which I didn't tell David about. I was discovered by one of the new guards responsible for the block. My husband managed to run away, but she caught me and noted the number that was on my arm. Later they called me to the entrance of the block and I told the truth, that I was with my husband, that he worked in the "commando" and that I wanted to see him and find out how he was. I didn't inform on the woman who was in charge who had helped me.

It is hard to describe the beatings that I consequently suffered. After that they put me in solitary confinement for three days. The solitary confinement cell was my size, I couldn't sit down in it, I could only stand. Three days went by without any food or water. I propped myself up against the wall but the wall was frozen since it was snowing outside. I literally froze; if I had had to stay there any longer, I wouldn't have survived.

After three days of standing, or leaning against the wall in solitary confinement, the same woman who had discovered me at the meeting with my husband took me out of solitary confinement and immediately poured a bucket of cold water over me. I don't know how I endured; this was one of the moments in which I felt myself walking between life and death. Luckily the same woman responsible for my block, Eta Gutman whom I knew from before, instructed me to stay inside the block. She helped me a lot and promised me that as long as she was alive, I didn't have to worry, that she would help me and that I too would prevail. I don't know why I aroused her sympathy;

she was very cruel to other people. She used to say to me: "Carla, I can see that you don't push, you are a decent woman, you are married and you are from Holland. I want you to stay alive.

She told me to stay inside the block, this way it would be easier for me. I helped to clean the block, which was also very hard labour. The work was at night; we had to empty the buckets into which the women prisoners emptied their bodily waste. It was awful to see how they dragged themselves around, how they fought for a slice of bread and how they all lay down together on the hard wooden boards, their bodies piled one on top of the other as if all of them were one. During the day, when the rest of the women were out of the block, I would lie down on the wooden boards and get bitten by the lice.

This was the most difficult period in Birkenau for me. I saw all the night's horrors; I watched as all the transports reached Auschwitz; I remember a transport of Hungarian Jews. In the transport were a bride and groom who were caught in the middle of their wedding, together with all their guests, and among them were many children. They were led directly to the gas chambers, and later to the crematoriums; I saw this with my own eyes. One night I saw how they took out all the gypsies from the "Gypsies Block", which was close to our block, and led them down their last path.

One night I saw a whole pile of corpses, they were laid down like wooden logs, one corpse to the right and another corpse to the left. For a long time our minds were numb to the scenes of horror and nobody was moved by this, everyone was alienated from each other. All of a sudden, I saw that a woman who had died was still wearing shoes that were in tact on her feet. I wanted them, but my conscious tormented me; how could I take shoes from a dead woman? But I myself had been walking around barefoot in the snow, my toes frozen. I thought to myself: Maybe these shoes would save my life, maybe because of them I would survive? The shoes could no longer be of any use to the woman who lay there, whereas for me... I shall never forget what I felt at that moment; I am very sensitive to these things. I got closer to the pile of corpses; I took the shoes off her corpse and cleaned the lice off of them. The shoes were frozen hard from the cold; I held them in my hands agitated, deliberating with myself and tormented, asking myself and also responding: "Carla is this really you? Are you capable of doing this? Think Carla, think, if you don't take them, surely somebody else will. Is your life worth less than the life of any other prisoner?"

The penny dropped, and against all my principles, I took the shoes that I had taken off the feet of the dead woman a few minutes earlier, for myself. In retrospect I believe that those shoes did indeed save my life. Since then, every time that I put on a pair of shoes, those shoes from Birkenau come back to haunt me and I can see them before my eyes. Today, I am missing a toe from each foot; these were removed surgically after the war in Holland because of the gangrene that had spread in them. Today, I am convinced that I owe my life to that dead woman and her shoes.

This is a subject which has often come back to me and burnt in my mind, I have thought about and analysed the circumstances over and over, becoming more and more confident that unless the Germans had descended to the lowest spiritual and human level possible, they would not have succeeded in changing the psychological state of other human beings-one expression of which was to steal footwear from the dead and use for one's own need.

I could tell you about many moments like these, but it is very difficult for me. I am very sensitive about all the ways in which I survived in Birkenau and to forget is impossible, whether one wants to or not, to forget is absolutely impossible. At any given moment some picture arises from the death camp. I experience associations from there all the time. For example, when I go to a supermarket and see such an abundance of food products, I remember how I was starving and desperate for a single piece of bread in Birkenau. When I see chickens on a grill, it brings up a whole world of terrifying associations for me, of how they burnt the corpses there.

From my transport nobody survived, and I don't have anyone with whom I can talk about it, and I can't forget the horrors. All the chimneys of Birkenau rise before my eyes, I can recall the smell of the burnt corpses all the time, and I see myself standing there. I don't know what the fate of Eta Gutman was, or if she survived...

At a later stage I asked Eta Gutman to send me to work outside, since I could no longer continue to work in the block at nights.

When the Russians started to get closer to Auschwitz, the Germans tried to destroy all evidence of their crimes. Their aim was that by the time the Russians arrived there would be no trace left of the gas chambers and the crematoriums, but they did not succeed. The Russians' advance was faster than expected. The Germans started to destroy the crematoriums. They sent us to do this work for them. We got closer to the crematoriums and started to demolish the walls, and then the real horror was revealed. We shivered to the bone when confronted by the scenes that were inside them.

We knew that there had been a heroic uprising of the "Sonderkommando" in Birkenau, in 1944. There was this one German officer, by the rank of "Sturm Fuhrer", I can still see him right before my eyes; a transport arrived from Danzig and among them was a famous actress (I knew her name, but I can't recall it now). The German officer ordered her to get undressed and go "take a shower". While saying, "I will not go to take a shower", the actress drew a pistol and shot him. She kept the pistol because she knew what was in store for her. The Sonderkommando threw the Nazi among the dead, and the Germans used to say that he had been thrown into the furnaces while he was still alive.

On that same night, there was a call to the head-count field all of a sudden. The members of the "Sonderkommando" cut the barbed wire fences and started to run; about half of those who fled were shot dead. It is hard to describe the fear that spread among us; they said that every tenth person would be brought before a firing squad, but in the end, they punished us severely, but didn't shoot us. When we returned to the blocks we experienced another tragic moment. The "Aryan" female guards said: "We thought that none of you would come back alive, because today it doesn't stink, today Jews aren't being burnt". They beat us intensively, took our bread, we thought that all of us would be executed…

In just a few words, this was the rebellion of the "Sonderkommando"; what happened to them afterwards … how many of them were shot … I do not know.

There was another moment that any prisoner who survived Birkenau will never forget. It was the heroic death of Mela Zimtebaum, my best friend. She was the most beautiful, good hearted and courageous young woman. She worked in a German office, where she met a non-Jewish young man, a charming man, and together they ran away from the camp. There was a rumour that she was caught in Krakow and we were told that she would be brought back to Birkenau, and indeed she was brought back to us. We saw how Mela passed through the camp's gate, pulled out a razor blade from her hair, cut her wrists and shouted "Don't forget me!" If I remember rightly, but I am not sure of this, she also had time to cut the face of the "Sturm-Fuhrer" that led her in. Even if I wanted to verify the details, I no longer have with whom to do so; I don't have any acquaintances from the first transport, nor from the second, nor from the third; I have never met any person from those who were with me in the camp.

I was in Birkenau till 18th January 1945. When the Russians got closer the camp was evacuated. The room where the bread was kept and the room where the sugar was kept were opened, and anybody who could took some food for the way. It was a horrible "Death March". Outside it was bitterly cold, it was the month of January in Poland, we were wearing torn clothes, reticent, thousands of "Ka-Tsetniks" [concentration camp prisoners], who were being marched out of Birkenau. I remember one woman who couldn't march; she was shot on the spot. I can see her before my eyes.

My feet were frozen, truly, I had a pair of shoes but I couldn't wear them, I walked on. A few girlfriends and I supported one another, and heeded each other: "Endure at any cost; otherwise you will be left in the middle of the road". How long the march was, I can't remember. How we managed to keep standing in that death march, I cannot describe. It was a horrible experience for me and for all the others.

We saw people falling in the snow, those who were physically unable to catch up with the other marchers; the SS ran to them immediately and shot them. Every shot caused my body to tremble. Shots could be heard all the time and the road was full of bodies lying in a pool of their own blood in the snow. And those of us who were still alive were being led on and on.

At a later stage they loaded us onto open wagons; we were lying one on top of the other, people were defecating on each other, without a drop of water or a slice of bread... We were frozen from the cold and they had loaded us on, stacked one on top of the other, as if we were logs. In the end we reached Ravensbruck. A place that was also terrible, it is impossible to describe what it was like there. Ravensbruck had high walls, surrounded by filth, lice and flies. We lay down on the ground and those who were already there attacked us, as if we had come to rob them of their last slice of bread, as if we had come there of our own free will… everybody was hungry, there was filth everywhere, really hell on earth.

Yehudah Dov (Bear)

Hanna: Do not forget my dear brother Yehudah Bear. The Poles informed on him to the Gestapo, and they, wanted to make a spectacle of him. He knew only too well what the meaning of that was; therefore, instead of going through being tortured he preferred to take his own life. He slit his wrists and then bit by bit, as the blood run out of his arteries, so too did his life run out, until finally he breathed his last breath. The Gestapo, who stood by and watched, said to him: "Die slowly you dirty Jew, it would be a pity to waste a bullet on you", and laughed.

Yaakov: The Germans were looking for me and instead they caught my brother Yehudah, who resembled me, together with our friend Edek. They were suspected of being Jews and they were led to a detention cell in Dembinka's forest, close to the district's capital Hrubieszow.

My brother Yehudah and I, knowing the Germans and what they were capable of, used to carry razor blades in our pocket- as the thing that we feared most was being tortured by them. We knew that if we were caught by the Germans and they decided to torture us, we would slit our wrists and end our life in this way.

When Yehuda Bear and Edek where caught by the Gestapo and taken into custody, Yehudah panicked; he was afraid of the torture, moreover he was afraid that during the interrogations he would give me up. Therefore, before it would be impossible to do so, he took out the razor blade, cut his own veins and started bleeding to death. The Germans didn't take care of him; they just threw him out of the custody cell, outside into the snow. The Ukrainians who saw this abused him terribly too. For three days he was moribund in agony until he died. All this happened about two months before the Russians liberated us.

Edek was sent to a doctor to be checked to see whether he was a Jew. He was checked by the doctor and they were told that: "He's not a Jew" after which he was released. Edek couldn't believe his good luck, but he didn't ask any questions. When the war was over and the Russians arrived, Edek approached the doctor and ask him: "How come you told them that I wasn't a Jew?" The doctor told him: "I too am a Jew." It turned out that this doctor had saved many Jews. The awful thought that, if Yehudah had not committed suicide, in all likelihood he would have been saved as well, is unbearable and haunts me to this very day.

Yehudah died in my place, he sacrificed his life for mine and died instead of me. [Father blamed himself his entire life for the death of Yehudah, and he never forgave himself for this; every time he talked about his brother Yehudah he had tears in his eyes]. I was caught between the lions' teeth; I had passed through the seven chambers of hell and by a miracle I had been saved from the claws of the predators; and here, I am a free man! I wanted to be reunited with Yehudah. I arrived in Husynne at the end of the war, where Edek brought me the worst news of all; Yehudah had

perished in Hrubieszow.

The war was close to being over and I thought and believed that if we had survived it up until now, that we would get through it safely. I had never believed that a storm could come and uproot one of us. How could an oak such as he has fallen? How had his life been cut short? I went into shock.

Everything that I had gone through during the war hadn't broken me, like what had happened to my brother broke me. He was close to me, heart and soul. As children we were loving friends, I admired him. I took this awful news very badly; I couldn't digest what had happened. The pain burned within me; the feeling of a missed opportunity was overwhelming. The shock was so great that for three days I couldn't get a word out of my mouth, I became mute. Later, my speech slowly started to come back to me.

The Moments of Liberation

Yaakov: It was on Sunday 20th January 1945, at 13:30. The forces of the Red Army entered the village. I stood there in disbelief; I pinched myself and wondered, "Is this really happening or am I dreaming? Are what my eyes seeing real or just a passing vision?" When I understood that we were being liberated I felt as if an electric current was rushing through my whole body.

I had spent my time in this last village as a simple Polish worker, up until the Russians arrived. They encircled the area, killed all the Germans and let us wander around freely.

Until the Russians came and liberated us I was like a predator; my senses were heightened and I could detect any rustle, any threat of danger. On one hand, with my head held high and my heart uplifted, I was ready to fight and do anything in order to stay alive. On the other hand, I was bitter and behaved like a wild animal. I held a pistol on one hand and a knife in the other and my teeth were ready to gnaw the throat of anyone from the Gestapo I came across (which happened on more than one occasion). As soon as I could feel my freedom, suddenly new blood started to flow through my body. I became as gentle as a lamb, I felt I had returned to being human again, relaxed and merciful, with the emotions of a human being. "And you turned my wailing into dancing".

When the Russian soldiers entered the town, I came out towards them. I wanted to greet them and talk to them. But they were set on carrying out their mission - to catch any German imposters and wipe them out. They suspected me too; they asked me to present my documents and started to interrogate me and ask me questions. I thought that the war was behind me, but they caught me by surprise. They decided that I too was a German who was impersonating a Pole, and they wanted to execute me following a field trial. Then a Russian officer approached me and asked: "Are you a Jew?", and I answered: "I, a Jew? I'm a Pole" and the officer said to me: "This is the only thing that can save you now", so I answered in a weak voice and said, "Yes, I am a Jew". I did not have any choice but to roll down my trousers in order to prove to him that I was indeed a Jew. Then the officer said to me: "You can tell me freely that you are a Jew. I am a Jew too, you needn't be afraid anymore to say that you are a Jew". It was the first time that the fact that I was a Jew had saved my life.

Hanna: One night a heavy bombardment started. It was on the night of 13th February 1945; it was the most horrible night. The sky lit up like a fir tree full of sparks. [This was the American and English bombardment of Dresden; 1,300 heavy bombers dropped 3,900 tons of bombs and incinerator bombs in four waves of bombardments. It lasted for three days, from13th-15th February 1945.The number of casualties was about twenty thousand souls, most of them whom were women and children, and about eighty five percent of the city's buildings, over an area of thirty four square kilometres in the city's centre, were completely destroyed.] How can I describe this? Buildings collapsed like playing cards towers. From a beautiful city, Dresden became a city that buried its dead under the rubble. The "Lazarett" was closed.

Ida ran off in one direction and Anton in another. I stayed in the garden with Roland and some other people from our house. The following morning Ida came back with Anton, they picked us up and together we ran away to the mountains not far from Dresden, where we waited until the bombardment ceased. It seemed that every bomb had an address with a name, written on it by fate. It seemed that fate had forgotten our names and that that was how we stayed alive.

Yaakov: While they were running away from the city that was under attack, at a certain moment they had nowhere to go. So they stopped, and trembling with fear clung to a wall of one of the buildings that they saw. That building was bombed, and by some miracle, the entire building collapsed to one side and only the wall that they had clung to remained standing, and so they were saved. **Hanna:** On the 8th of May 1945 the war was over. The Germans signed the final surrender agreement. We saw the Russian Army enter. It was like a dream. We came down from the mountains to greet and talk to them. We looked for someone who spoke Yiddish. Every soldier who had a beard looked like a Jew to us. In the end we found someone who spoke Polish, he was a Polish Jew. He warned us not to return to Poland, but to go to a faraway country. Seeing as before the war some of our family had moved

to Holland, we started thinking about going there.

Carla: After a few days in Ravensbruck they took us to Razev, another type of hell, but here we could already smell the approaching liberation in the air. Here we could start hoping that the day when our troubles would be behind us was not far off. Indeed, at that time, it still seemed like a dream, a fantasy, but we could see the anxiety and nervousness that prevailed among the Germans, who were starting to lose their senses and confidence. They thought that if they would hide among us they would be protected from the Russian conqueror. They understood that the Russians were advancing like a storm and we even heard them say that if the Russians reached us they would rather slit their wrists than fall into their hands.

We were a small group of six women; myself, four Czech women and one Hungarian, we decided to run away to the forest, since we feared that the Germans wanted to march us on further. We turned towards the forest having made the decision that whatever happened we would make a run for it.

While escaping we entered a building that the Germans had evacuated a short time earlier. There was a feeling of relief; we no longer saw the guards in the towers. We continued to run on further and further away. One of the Czech women had said to me: "Carlcz'ka, come with us" and I ran away with them. We burst through the building that was on the way, we didn't even look for food, we just headed straight for the forest. On the way we came across a dying man, these were his last moments, he was unable to tell us who he was or where he was from, and after a few minutes he died. We dug a grave, took a bottle and put a note in it, in which we wrote that we had been there on that day, and that the man that we had found had passed away on that same day. He was a Jew. We buried him there.

We were very hungry, the bullets were whistling over our heads, these were shots from the German side. We felt that we were close to where the fighting was taking place. We came across a pit and jumped into it. Suddenly a woman came out of the pit and said to us: "Girls, I can hear Russian." We lay down deep inside the pit. The woman was a Yugoslav partisan, not a Jewess. She had been through a long and difficult journey. She told us that she had taken a young Jewish woman under her patronage but that the latter had not survived.

The Yugoslav partisan decided that she had to check where we were in relation to the front and what was happening around us. She snuck out that night. We spent the second day squashed together in the pit and very frightened. On the third day she came back and said in Russian: Girls, "Vas asvabdili" ["You are free"]. There was no limit to our happiness. It was easy to understand our joy. We came across the Russians and they told us: "Wait another day and a half, and then our tanks will arrive". I personally didn't believe them, but the partisan calmed me down and said: "We are in a safe place and we shall not move from here", and she was right.

We stayed there until one morning the Russian tanks arrived. The first Lieutenant whom we met was a Jew, he was very happy to meet us. The exited partisan climbed up the tank. He kissed us and said: "Don't be afraid, trust me. Go back to your homes; to the countries where you came from, but you have to be careful on the way." When he heard that I was from Holland, he insisted that I should not accept any alternative plan, but that I should go back home.

The Russian tanks continued to arrive and flow in. The Russian soldiers brought us to houses that the Germans had abandoned and told us: "Take whatever you want". I took only one dress and put it on; I did not touch anything else. I arrived in Amsterdam wearing that same dress.

After the Liberation

Yaakov: After the liberation I returned home, to my parent's house in Skulsk. It wasn't far away, but I had to get there on foot walking for many days and nights until I reached it. When I got there I was only to discover that over the six years of the war, the Poles who used to work for us before the war had taken over all our assets. They had robbed us of everything: our two houses, the old timber one and the new one that we built not long before the war, our large plot of land and the storehouse for the building materials. There were some young Polish women living in the new house; I wanted to sleep there and they wouldn't let me, they drove me out. I found out that they had taken over the rest of the Jewish houses as well, among others the house of Pola Gliksman.

I was hungry and thirsty; I asked people that I knew for some food and water. There was one Polish family that owned a bakery; they were the only ones to answer my plea. But there were others, who not only did they not want to give me anything, in fact wanted to see me dead. I looked straight into their eyes and asked them: "Have you no shame? After I fought in the Polish army and was a prisoner of war, after I survived the war, now you threaten to kill me?"

I wanted to put up a fight and repossess my assets, to get back everything which had been stolen from me; everything which my father and mother had worked for all their lives. I went to the police in Skulsk. Of course, they identified me as the son of Kotowski, but they didn't help me much. When I returned to my home, the Pole who had taken over my house had hurried and called together other Poles from the surrounding area, and they had come, armed with pitchforks, shovels and sticks, ready to kill me.

Yukev and Zabo, a childhood friend of ours (who later moved to live in the United States), also returned home. They heard that I was alive and that I had returned to Skulsk, so they came to see me. They started to talk to me in Yiddish; it sounded very strange to me, so strange and foreign that I reprimanded them: "Why are you speaking to me in Yiddish?" they laughed and asked me: "Yaakov, don't you know Yiddish anymore?" I told them that this was not my language anymore and that I was no longer a Jew. For three years I had lived like a Christian, behaved and thought like a Christian, so much so that I was unable to speak Yiddish anymore, moreover I didn't respond when Yiddish was spoken to me and I felt that I no longer had the will to be a Jew. They continued to talk to me, in Polish only, and then Yukev took me aside and spoke to me. He tried to bring me back to my senses; he explained to me that there was nothing that could change the fact that I was a Jew and that everything I had gone through had disheartened me and caused me to become distressed, and that now I needed to look for my way back...

Yukev could see what the Poles had done to me; and he knew that the farmers were getting closer with their pitchforks and that eventually they would kill me. He convinced me to run away with him: "Yaakov let's run away from here. After getting through the entire war alive, we might now be killed by the Poles if we don't." At the very last minute we escaped with our lives. I left everything behind and ran away with Yukev. He convinced me to come with him to Sompolno, where there were still a few Jews left together. The Memorial Day for the soldiers killed in battle from our county takes place in the month of June. May and June are the nicest months in Poland. All my Jewish

friends who had gone up the bridge that we built on the Warta River when we were young and came to the front with me did not return. Only my cousin
Yukev and I came home after the war.

Everything that I have told you up until now is no more than a fraction of what happened; it is just a drop in the ocean of what we went through and experienced; six stormy years in which in every second, of every minute, of every hour of every day, our lives were on the brink of an abyss. Six years, the chronicles which would take an entire life-time to give an account of.

Yukev: We lived in Sompolno until we heard that there were Poles there who belonged to anti-Semitic organizations such as AK [The Krajowa Army was an underground movement in Poland, whose members acted as partisans, and a lot of Jewish blood was spilt at their hands], who were hunting down Jews in order to kill them. The saga of our sufferings because we were Jews was not yet over. We discovered that even though the war had ended, the time for a peaceful and secure life had not yet come. I felt that nothing was tying me down to my childhood home anymore. Moreover, we were young and everyone was very mobile; Europe after the war was full of refugees who were wandering from place to place, looking for security and a livelihood. I decided to join them.

Yaakov: I decided to do what I had always dreamt of doing, which was to immigrate to the Land of Israel. For two thousand years Jews had prayed a few times a day: "And our eyes will watch when you return to Zion and to Jerusalem your city with mercy; you will return and you will gather us from the four ends of the earth, and you will bring us on eagles' wings ..."

I went to the kibbutz of Hashomer Hatzair in Lodz. It was a kibbutz run by the partisans who had fought the Germans; among the members of this kibbutz was also one Chaika Grossman, who years later became a Member of the Knesset. Immigration envoys from what was then Palestine arrived at the kibbutz in order to train people for immigration to the Land of Israel.

Below is a letter that I wrote to my sister Golda and my brother-in-law Chaim, who lived in Haifa:

Magenta, 26 October 1945

[Magenta is a town located near to Milan, in northern Italy. After the Second World War the Mossad established a transition camp for Jews there, who were getting ready for illegal immigration to the Land of Israel.]

I can't describe to you how happy I was when I received your first letter through kibbutz member Dorkin, who they all call Artsi here, he is an instructor at our kibbutz. You will probably soon get another three letters from me, which I have already sent. I sent my last letter with a "Tzabar" [native Israeli] instructor, who is also here on the kibbutz. He lives not far from Haifa and promised he would visit you and convey my regards to you in person. I believe that he will meet you even before my letter reaches you.

I also wrote a letter to the Jewish community in Amsterdam, enquiring about Carla's exact address now, since when I was in Sompolno in Poland, a niece of Ida's husband [Anton] told me that she was with Carla in Auschwitz, and that she had survived, so she must be together with her husband by now; I hope so, for her sake. As I have their address in Holland, I shall write them a letter today and also send one to America.

I had many doubts that Ida, Anton and even Carla were really alive; since I had corresponded with Yehudah Bear right up until he was caught…After he was shot the Germans found all the letters and pictures that he had in his possession. But fate would have it and they did indeed survive. Edek also survived but is now an orphan; he is the only one from his entire family who survived. At least one person from his family remained… May all of us, the survivors, live in peace and happiness, including the orphans and the misfortunate;

and even if just one person from a family survived, our beloved race will live on. I guess that is how it had to be; for those who perished nothing can now be done, they are no longer alive and we, the living, are compelled to go on and build our future, and to sprout new branches of our family trees.

Yesterday, when I got your letter, and even now as I am sitting here writing to you, tears are choking me and I want to burst out crying for those who will not get the same privilege as we will, knowing that in a few weeks or months we shall all meet. But where are Yehudah Bear, Father, Mother, Pola, Avraham and young Shulamit?

When I recall what I was told about the last minutes of Yehudah Bear's life, how bleeding to death in the German prison, he was thrown out on the street to die; I swear I shall never be able to forget the testimonies and my visions of him, not until I take my last breath. In my mind I was also present there and I saw how the murderers led him to his death. I could not help him because their intention was to kill me too; but let's leave that for another time. When we meet, you will hear enough about the troubles that we had, under what horrible conditions we went through the war, and what a great miracle it is that we survived.

I wish you "Mazal Tov" on the birth of your son Roni, from the depths of my heart. Arel'ka must certainly be a beautiful girl by now. I can recall how back home our deceased father and mother always used to cry whenever we received a letter from you, just as I am crying now; the tears are choking me up. May we not know any more sorrow, but only happy occasions and good news.

Please send me pictures of you and your beloved children as soon as possible, so that at least I may have you on paper, since I currently don't have any pictures left.

How is the Wilczynski family? [Uncle Avraham, Aunt Regina, and Cousin Rachel who live in Haifa]. Please ask them to put in a few words and also send me a picture; please send them greetings from me.

Do you get to meet Moishe Biederko, Gabrisz Rogorzynski or Tova Pretzel sometimes? I would ask that my beloved Zehava also write me a few words. I will end my letter to you here, because some soldiers have arrived, in a car that is leaving soon and I want to send the letter with them. Greetings to Uncle Avraham, Aunt Regina, Cousin Rachel and all my friends from Skulsk and Sompolno.

Blessings and Kisses, Yaakov, who misses you.

Hanna: After endless pleading and a lot of crying about everything that we had been through, we finally managed to get hold of a car. At that time having a car was something very valuable. Roland knew how to drive and we drove to the American border. The Americans took everything from us. They sent Roland and a few other French people who had travelled with us to a French refugee camp; and we were sent to a Polish refugee camp.

That night the Poles discovered that we were Jews and they wanted to kill us. We started to escape and were saved by a miracle; one of the refugees that had escaped with us told us that there was also a Jewish camp in the town we had come from. We turned in the town's direction and luckily there were also some Dutch people in that camp. After a lot of convincing, we left with them for Holland.

Carla: For a few days the Russians continued to guard us, since we were still in danger of being harmed. Soldiers could have kidnapped us at night, since it was still a time of war. A Jewish soldier approached us and said: "I shall stand by you and guard you because the situation is horrendous; there are many cases of women being attacked and many stories about the harm the Russians are doing to women in the various camps."

They also took us to work; we helped them in the kitchen and cleaning the buildings. We ate what they ate, pulses and sausage. My situation was difficult; I was Dutch and the question was how would

I get from there to the west? It was not simple at all.
What could one do?
The Russians took us with them until we met a group of French prisoners of war. I joined them since I knew that the minute, I reached France, Holland would be closer. The women I was with offered to take me to Czechoslovakia with them, the Hungarian to Hungary; I thanked them all and told them that I wanted to return to Holland, the country from where I was deported to Auschwitz.

The journey to Holland was hard; we were just two women, in a group of 40-50 French prisoners of war who had also recently been liberated. Among them was a Jew to whom I owe a lot of thanks as a woman. He saved me, since among the prisoners of war there were all types of people.

I wandered about for four weeks before I saw the Dutch border; but it was difficult to enter Holland. The authorities were afraid of epidemics and I have to admit that we were in a shocking state. They prevented our entry by force and it was impossible to continue onwards to Amsterdam. The border was closed and they kept us in various camps. In the end, as soon as it became possible, I boarded the first train to Amsterdam. It was on 2nd June 1945; I shall never forget that date. I reached a shelter for displaced Dutch people who were returning after the war.

I knew that there were still very good acquaintances and friends of mine living in Holland, non-Jews that I had left many valuables with. First, I managed to reach a Dutch family who were my friends. They received me with excitement and warmth which is hard to describe; they were real friends, devoted people. They gave me new clothes and food.

During my time in the camps the Germans used to force us to send postcards home; they also dictated the content of the postcards to us, making us say that we were in regular work camps etc. They hoped that we would write to other Jews and by this expose their addresses. I figured that if I wrote to other Jews I might do them harm, therefore I didn't; instead I wrote to non- Jews, knowing it wouldn't do them any harm. Consequently, I would write to these friends and they would respond. Their replies reached Birkenau. The Germans used to summon me to the post office building and let me read their letters; I was very happy that they replied to my postcards.

But my real aim was to reach my friends, the Baker family, as that was where I had left all my valuable things. It was not simple to reach them since there were no means of transport available. But eventually, after two days I managed to reach them; The Baker family smothered me with kisses.

On the day that we were deported from Amsterdam, it had been my friend's birthday. I had sent her a flower pot with a white flower as a present. She had looked after the flower throughout the three years that I had been absent. On the day I returned she said to me: "Carla, come to my garden, see, here is your flower; every year when the flower blossomed, it was a sign for me that Carla and David existed somewhere, that you were still alive and that the day would come when you would return to Amsterdam. Take your flower, our door is always open to you, here are all the things that belong to you, we didn't touch a thing." No item was missing; just imagine that she had cleaned and polished everything

for three years…

Then, I went to the house of some other friends of mine; she was a non-Jewish Dutch woman called Ini Vero Falm and he was a Dutch Jew that we had had trading relations with before the war. They also received me with great warmth; it is difficult to describe the love with which they surrounded me, they didn't let me leave and I ended up staying with them. Everything started to sort itself out and stabilise, but I had no peace of mind; I didn't know what the fate of my husband David was; was he still alive? And when they celebrated my friend's birthday, I was sad, David hadn't returned.

In retrospect it turned out that my husband was also in a shelter for displaced people who had returned to their homeland. He happened to meet an ex-worker from our factory by chance and he asked her if she had seen me. She told him that I was alive and that she had seen me on the roads. O-then David started looking for me. Where? At our mutual friends. He was also helped by a clerk who searched through all his papers until he managed to locate my name.

One morning, the house-maid of the family where I was being hosted at noticed a man, approximately in his thirties and who did not look 'normal' at all, approaching the door of the house. Agitated and frightened she called Ini, the landlady, and warned her that a poor miserable beggar had arrived at their door, and who knew what he wanted. Ini calmed her down and said that it was fine, and that she would go check on the man and see what he wanted.

I waited a while and noticed that Ini, my Christian friend, hadn't come back; it aroused my curiosity and I started to worry. I came out to the gate and saw Ini lying on the ground, and next to her stood a shocked man, dressed in rags. I approached him in Dutch and asked him what was the purpose of his coming to the house. He looked at me with a lot of concentration and he answered: "Carla, don't you recognise me, it's me David." I have to admit; the face had changed so much that I really didn't recognise my own husband. And all this time Ini had been lying on the ground unconscious; her husband who came to the gate was the first to ask: "David, is that you?" David had arrived at the house of our friends where I was staying.

How can I describe such an emotional meeting? there are no words. David my husband was in terrible condition; he didn't have any teeth and he weighed about 33-34 kilograms.

When the great excitement was over, they received David in their home as well, hosting us both with all their hearts. It was such a warm reception, there's nothing like it. And indeed, we stayed with them for 2-3 weeks. In this time David recovered and when he felt strong enough, we got a taxi and returned to our home.

We travelled to the house of some other friends of ours, where we had left what was left of all our possessions. Needless to say, David's clothes didn't fit him; everything was too big for his body's new dimensions, since he was only skin and bones. Later, we found our factory, which was returned to us and we started to rebuild our lives all over again, almost from scratch. My husband gradually recuperated and things started to return to normalcy. A son was born to us and we called him Carlos.

Carla, David and Carlos Lewenhoff

Jopie: In May 1945 the north of Holland was liberated. The Jewish community started to reorganise slowly. The remaining survivors of the Holocaust returned from the hell they had been through to their homes. In this way Aunt Carla returned from Auschwitz. After a few weeks, Uncle David Lewenhoff, her husband, also returned. Their meeting was very emotional since they hadn't seen each other, or known if either of them was still alive, for such a long time. They started to rehabilitate their lives from the trauma of the war, and the assets that had been taken from them when they were deported from Holland were returned to them. When they heard that I was still alive and that I was in Amsterdam they wanted to adopt me. And indeed, I moved in and started to live with them, thanks to an organization which took care of the guardianship issues.

One day, while I was at Aunt Carla's, a letter arrived from the town of Davos in Switzerland. There was a rehabilitation house there for people who had tuberculosis. The letter was from Avraham Sar-Louis, the son of the Rabbi of Amsterdam, who had been a friend of my father's. He had been sent to this rehabilitation house in Switzerland during the war, so that he wouldn't infect other people, and by some miracle he had been saved. After his recovery he immigrated to Israel and worked at the foreign office. Eventually, he was sent as a Consul of Israel to Uruguay, and there he met Hanna and Carla.

Following the letter that I received from him I decided to immigrate to Palestine. To this end I stayed on a farm in Holland for a year; there I learnt to speak Hebrew and about agriculture, and I became a Zionist. During that period, before 1948, the United Nations declared what was to be the Partition Plan for Palestine, and Zionist organizations wanted to bring as many children as possible from Europe to Israel, so that they would be present during the establishment of The State of Israel.

I travelled to my village to take leave of the family that had taken care of me. The family's mother tried to convince me not to immigrate to Palestine; she was very worried, but my decision was final.

We received Dutch certificates, travelled by train to Paris, and from there we immigrated on "Aliya Bet" - a clandestine immigration. On the way we came down through the South of France; at that time, Polish, Hungarian and our Dutch youth groups were established. We all boarded a ship with forged documents and travelled to Italy, Port Said and from there to Haifa. In Haifa the "Hagana" [the Jewish underground in British Mandatory Palestine] sent people to the ship, and their new certificates were given to us.

Epilogue

Yaakov: We travelled to Italy with the other kibbutz members from Lodz; there a small ship called "Hanna Senesh" was awaiting us. On this ship we travelled to the Land of Israel on what was known as "Aliya Bet."

This was in the winter of 1945. The ship was small and rickety, the captain of which was an Italian. The sea was rough and for about two weeks the ship was tossed from side to side, like a nutshell in the windswept waters. Many people boarded the ship and it was very overcrowded. We were not used to sea voyages and people got seasick, in addition to being afflicted with other diseases.

There was sufficient food on the ship but not enough water. We were thirsty all the time. There were wine barrels on the ship; those who couldn't resist the temptation drank the wine, got drunk and vomited. It was awful.

On Christmas Eve, the commanders of the Hagana appealed to the residents of Nahariya with a strange request; they asked them to invite all the British soldiers who were in the area to a festive meal in their homes. They asked the hosts to make sure that there would be good food and plenty of wine on the table, so that their guests would get drunk; and so, it was…

That evening, on the 25th of December 1945, while the British soldiers dined in the company of their local hosts, the unauthorised ship "Hanna Senesh" arrived on the shores of Nahariya, carrying 252 illegal immigrants. The ship anchored close to the rocky shore; and the beach was clear of any soldiers. The illegal immigrants were taken off the ship quickly and led by the young men of the "Pal Yam" [the Sea Company] and the Hagana to the settlements in the surrounding area.

In the morning, when the soldiers returned to their duties, they discovered the abandoned illegal ship and on it an improvised flag with the inscription: "Consider this one of the gravestones for our six million brothers and sisters who perished, and a symbol of disgrace for the British Government."

[The flag with the inscription can be found in "The Navy and Ha'apala Museum", at the southern entrance to Haifa].

Since the ship ended up beached on a sandbank it was necessary to take captain Ansaldo and all his crew off the ship and smuggle them to one of the settlements in the area, since if they would have been caught by the British, they would have been arrested. Therefore, they were smuggled to kibbutz Yagur.

At a party that took place a few days later on the kibbutz, Ansaldo, the Italian captain of the ship, delivered a very moving speech and declared: "I left on this voyage in return for a fee; from this point on I shall continue to do my job without pay."

The poet Nathan Alterman, who also witnessed the operation, was invited to the event by the then commander of the "Palmach" [The elite force of the Hagana], Yitshak Sadeh. In his column in the "Davar" newspaper of those times, called "The Seventh Column", he saluted captain Ansaldo with his famous poem: "Response to an Italian Sea Captain, Following a Night of Disembarkation".

Response to an Italian Sea Captain

Words: Nathan Alterman Translation: Marie Syrkin

The wind lashed the sea, and the sea lashed the ship:
Yet the task was completed, holy Moses!
We drink to you, Captain, and lift the glass high:
We'll meet again on these waters.

No Lloyds would insure your small, secret craft,
Nor the perilous struggle it wages:
But though in the ship's log no record be kept,
We'll chart it in history pages.

This frail, hidden fleet, grey and silent, will be
The subject of song and of story:
And many a captain, who hears of the tale,
Will envy you, Captain, your glory.

The night hid the battle with wave and with tide,
But our lads than the storm-wind were stronger:
Oh, Captain, you saw how from ship to the shore
Each swam with a refugee on his shoulder.

A toast to the darkness that swooped on the ship,
And crouched on the long lights that sought her:
Oh, Captain, God-speed to the small, wooden, boats,
God-speed to these ships on the water!

A toast to the lads that took up the fight
And made it their peoples Trafalgar:
They turn each frail ship to a mailed man-of-war:

This ship is of steel-It will conquer.

Years to come-you'll sipping a glass of mulled wine,
Or quaffing a draught that is stronger:
Then you will smile, smoke your pipe, and shake your grey head,
And think of the days you were younger.

You'll remember past deeds, and say to your friends:
"I've seen much, but, by Santa Maria:
I'll never forget the night of the chase
When we sped towards Nahariya".

Then we'll tell you: "The gates of the land are open!
They are so for quite some time now, thanks God!
Open by the lads who clambered aboard
And carried ashore their precious load".

Then You'll chuckle and whisper:
"So nothing availed: neither radar, nor destroyers to block our way".
You'll curse in Italian and finish your glass
And the lights throughout the port will fade away.

That's how it will be! So, facing the lashing wind
a toast to the danger and hard work of today
Oh, Captain, God-speed to the small wooden boats,
God-speed to the ships making their way!

The people who were taken off the boat were exhausted from the continuous tossing and turning of the ship from side to side on its journey, and there were also people who didn't know how to swim on board. The men of the Hagana and the Pal Yam carried them off the ship on their shoulders. I too was exhausted, someone pulled me over his shoulders and asked me who I was and where I was from. I said that I was Yaakov Eliezer Kotowski from Skulsk in Poland. For a moment it seemed like he choked up when he heard my answer. When I asked him for his name, I discovered to my great surprise that he was Eliezer Kotowski from Haifa. This was how I found out that my cousin on my father's side, who was already living in the country, was the one who carried me off the boat and over his shoulders. This of course was another cause for great excitement.

I was sent to kibbutz Beit Oren, where I spent the night. In the morning I received new certificates and I travelled to my sister Golda in Haifa; I became a citizen of Palestine. On that day my dream to immigrate to the Land of Israel came true.

I volunteered for the Hagana. We didn't have enough ammunition, so we used to fill barrels with stones and roll them down the Carmel Mountain to the downtown area; the noise used to frighten the Arabs and they would run away.

I joined the fire brigade in Haifa for work and I also became a member in their orchestra. We gave concerts and had a regular audience that would come to listen to us. One day, a beautiful young lady of British origin who had many suitors sat in the audience. From the first time that I set eyes on her I knew that she would be my wife. With a lot of work, I managed to "get rid" of all her British suitors, and she did indeed become my beloved wife, Yael Jessie Chinn Kotowski.

In February 1948 I started to work as a collector. At that time the State couldn't finance the fire brigade, so it was decided that we would collect contributions. Then, another dark period in our history fell upon us, a period which is surely well documented in the chronicles of the War of Independence of the State of Israel. In every corner, death lay in wait for us, as we were threatened by the barrels of the Arabs' guns. Day after day I would leave for the "Krayot" [the towns on the outskirts of Haifa] and Neve Sha'anan to make my collections, not knowing if I would return alive come evening.

I asked myself: Was this real? Or was it all a dream? I, a person who had been through six years of the Shoah, who had once dreamt of giving a year of his life in return for a single slice of bread, or of surrendering myself to the devil in exchange for water to quench my thirst; six years of burning, slaughtering and suffocating six million Jews…Was it possible to believe that after six years of the darkest, thickest dark clouds, that had hidden the beauty of the sun and cast a shadow like " darkness had prevailed over the surface of the deep"; six years during which I cannot count the number of miracles that had happened to me…Was it possible that, I had torn open a small window? And like a bolt of lightning through the clouds blackened by the mountain of destruction, I had managed to dredge myself up from the ruins and destruction, and to sprout anew the branches that had been cut down? From my weary, dry bones I had raised a second generation of the "Oaks of Mamreh and Cedars of the Lebanon". I succeeded in bringing forth, may God bless them, sons and daughters, grandsons and granddaughters; they are "the branch of my planting, the work of my hands, that I may be glorified."

When I came to the Land of Israel, I started to build my family nest:

The first expression of my power was my firstborn son, Efri [Efraim Yitshak]; his name symbolizes the ashes ("efer") of my father, Yitshak Efraim, a person who pursued peace and the love of mankind. When I look at Efri, I often see my brother Yehudah.

My firstborn daughter, Tova [Tova Gitel], carries the name of my mother, who was very beautiful, kind, noble and gentle.

And last but not least, my youngest daughter, Dovit [Dovit Yehudit], carries the name of my brother, Yehuda Dov (bear), who saved my life by his death it is indeed a miracle that I am here.

Efri, Tova and Dovit Pedatsur (Kotowski)

In 1957 we changed the name Kotowski to Pedatsur [pronounced: Peda-tsur]; my sisters asked me not to, since I was the only one left from the family who carried the Kotowski name, and there was no one else left to commemorate this name; but they lived abroad and I lived in Israel, and at that time people changed their names to a Hebrew name, and so did I.

I chose this name from the Bible, from the book of Numbers, chapter seven, clause fifty-four: "Gamaliel the son of Pedatsur, prince of the children of Manasseh", since "My God, the Rock, my saviour!", "gamal li" [delivered me] and "pada oti" [redeemed me] from hell; and also, for my brother Yehudah, who redeemed me by his death.

Having come to the end of my tribulations and reached a state of tranquillity, as our birds started to leave the nest, the magnificent tree of our family was yet again cut down; the pillar of fire that illuminated our home stopped burning. [Unfortunately, our mother died of cancer when she was only fifty-four years old]. "Alas for those who are gone and no longer to be found." During the holocaust I was strong as a cliff, hard as a rock; but after the awful tragedy that befell me, I completely fell apart. It only happened two months ago and my strength has all dissipated, and it has become hard for me to tolerate any agitation or small insult. My life back home was free of any worries, the serenity and the quiet lulled me to sleep, and every morning at five o'clock the twittering of the turtledoves and the trees which knocked at the

glass panels of my window, awoke me.

And we should not forget the interpretation of the verse from "Song of Songs": "My beloved is gone down to his garden, to the beds of spices, to feed in the gardens, and to gather lilies"; Meaning: The holy one, blessed be he, has gone down to his garden and picked the best and dearest lily from our beds of spices; when she was still young, he took her to him and extinguished the pillar of fire that illuminated our home

And I, the youngest of them all, was lucky enough to see the second generation come forth, that they might cheer up their old grandfather;from my offspring came the first-born granddaughter, our dearest diamond, the magnificent crown, Anat Yael. Like a rosebud that can be found in the morning watch, the droplets of dew from Mount Hermon quench her thirst - and her laughter is as bright as the sunrise. There are many charming and beautiful daughters of Israel, but you have surpassed them all.

And to Yehiel [Hilik]: You should be overjoyed; it is your good fortune that you were born to the last generation of subjugation and the first generation of redemption, in the most beautiful days of our history. May you grow for us, as an oak on the banks of flowing waters.

Yael Jessie Chinn

Yael and Yaakov on their wedding day

[Two years passed and father got re-married to a woman who he had met by the name of Fania Frankel; she was a math's teacher at the comprehensive school in Be'er Sheba. He asked me (Dovit) where I would like to live - whether to continue living in Kiryat Ata or to move and live with them in Be'er Sheba. I decided to move and live with them. Father was married to Fania for approximately twenty years and we conducted a normal family life with the members of her family. We celebrated the festivals and happy events together and father left many written blessings, which he wrote specially for these occasions].

Do not look at me as the eldest of the family, since I carry on my shoulders six years of "Shoah", of suffering and bitterness. And I became betrothed to my country with tribulations and love. And when I sit here in the bosom of my happy, joyful and lovely family I am cheerful, happy and I feel good. But then visions from my time in the Diaspora pass before my eyes; visions of the young people of Israel, who went to battle against the Germans, as soldiers in the Polish army, and those who fought as partisans for the freedom of the Jewish people and do not have the privilege of being here among us. By their deaths they gave us life and liberty. And at the time that: "You removed the burden from my shoulders; in my distress I called you and you rescued me from death". Let us not forget them.

[Father fell ill with Alzheimer's, and when he lost his orientation he was moved to an old-age home in Safed. He passed away in 1993 at the age of 82.]

Hanna: In Holland I was reunited with my sister Carla and her husband David, both who had survived three years in Auschwitz. Carla told us about the tragedy that had befallen our sister Pola, her husband Avraham and their daughter Shulamit during the war, and that they had perished in the holocaust. Ida and Anton Piotrowski also came to Holland.

In Holland we started a new life; it was hard since Holland was completely destroyed after the war. I met Yitshak Krzywanowski there, who was a holocaust survivor like me; he had lost all his family in the holocaust, including his wife and two children. Naturally he didn't want to get married again, and of course he didn't want to raise a new family; but I, who had never been married and didn't have any children, convinced him to marry me. In 1947 we got married and in 1949 we had a son, his name is Menachem Mendel Krzywanowski, called Menno for short.

We lived in Holland until the Korean War broke out, and then in 1953 we decided to immigrate to Montevideo in Uruguay, together with David and my sister Carla. We lived in Uruguay for a number of years and in 1962 my husband Yitshak passed away.

Following this, I decided to immigrate to Israel and in 1963 Menno and I made Aliya. In the beginning we lived in Kfar Ata, close to my brother Yaakov. At a later stage I met my second husband, Zeev Gonsiorowicz, who was from Czestochowa in Poland; he too was a holocaust survivor and both of us were widowers. We got married in 1967 and Menno and I moved to live with Zeev in Tel Aviv.

Hanna and Yitshak at their wedding. Ida is whipping away a tear

Right to left: Ida, Hanna the bride and Carla

When I reached Israel, I became a member of the Organization for Ex-Konins; it was established by the survivors of the city of Konin and its surroundings, from Israel and abroad. We collected small sums of money and erected a monument in memory of all those who had perished in Konin and its surroundings in the Holon cemetery. We also engraved the name of our town on a memorial plaque in the Chamber of the Holocaust in Yad Va Shem.

[Our aunt Hanna lived happily with Zeev until she passed away in 2005 at the age of 88.]

Carla: In Europe, the winds of war started to blow again; this time the Korean War broke out. We could also feel the unsettled atmosphere in Holland. We were afraid to take any risks again; we had already learnt from our bitter experience. A relative who we were hosting, who had come from Uruguay for a visit, tried to convince us to leave Holland and immigrate to Uruguay. So, we seriously started to consider immigrating to South America. We got passports, gradually sold our assets and prepared ourselves for the journey.

I was not excited by the idea of leaving Holland for an unknown country, somewhere in South America, without knowing the language. What would we do there? But steps had been taken and there was no turning back. We left Holland in 1953. I can't forgive myself for that uncalculated step; I regretted it all my life. When we reached Uruguay, the situation was not especially pleasant; life there was not like in Holland.

We opened a shop for women's clothes, and as happens in life, according to a Yiddish proverb: "When comes the bread [Broit] – comes death [Toit]". As our situation got better, my husband passed away; it was 1966.

After the death of my husband I continued to manage the shop; not much time passed and in 1967, the Six Days War broke out in Israel. My son Carlos didn't want to stay in Uruguay, he wanted to go to Israel and join the I.D.F, and as other young men did, he left everything and went to Israel.

I had family in Israel, therefore I decided to sell the shop and in 1968 I made Aliya. In Israel the atmosphere I encountered was very different. I made contact with an organisation called "Sh'erit ha-Pletah" [Survivors of the Holocaust]; through them I met Zalman Marchak, who knew my family from before the war, and I got married again. He too was an Auschwitz survivor. After the war he had immigrated to the United States, he came to Israel for a visit and we got married in 1969.

During that period a trial took place against a Polish murderer who was active in Birkenau, his name was Willi Szawacki. The name was known to me from the camp and I remembered who he was. I felt that I had to testify against him otherwise my conscience would give me no peace. I was invited to testify against him in a trial that took place in Germany and I agreed without any hesitation. My husband was against my going to give testimony, but I was determined to go, and so I did.

I presented myself at the police station in Israel and told them all that I knew about the murderer and his iniquities in Auschwitz. I attested to the facts that the subject was a sadist, who hated and murdered children, a Pole of German origin. He took part in the liquidation of the Gypsies' camp. In any place he could do harm, he did. I testified that he was a despicable murderer, and I knew of all his crimes.

When I gave my testimony in the police station, I was told that a lawyer from Germany would come and that I would also have to tell him everything that I knew about that despicable murderer. I swore to keep the rest of my strength in order to bring him to justice. When the German lawyer came, I gave him my testimony and it was agreed that they would invite me to the trial of Szawacki that would take place in Frankfurt.

I was the only witness in the trial on the prosecution's side. The Judges asked me when I had been expelled from Holland to Auschwitz, under which circumstances I had known Szawacki, had I seen how he slaughtered people with my own eyes, etc. I declared that I had indeed seen him there and told them everything I knew about his crimes.

The trial was an unbearable experience for me. The revolting murderer sat not far from me, dressed elegantly like a British Lord. During the testimony I experienced everything all over again; the same scenes from Birkenau came up before my eyes. I was so agitated and nervous that when they showed me a map of Birkenau, I couldn't even point out the location of my block...

During the trial I looked at the faces of the panel of judges who sat around the [court's] presidential table. They all listened politely, but with indifference. It was difficult for me to withstand the situation, but I didn't lose my concentration. Next to me sat a translator from Israel, I told him how I felt and I answered all the questions that were directed at me. Deep inside myself I decided that I would not shed a tear, that I should stand erect and not give them the pleasure of seeing me weep. This may have given them some satisfaction; I decided that I would not break down.

At some point there was a recess. The Judges left to consult. The advocate who had taken my testimony in Israel was not there, as it was forbidden for him to be present at the trial. Later, I finished my testimony and I left the hall. When I left the court hall, I bumped into Szawacki. I asked him: "What did you do?" He said "Excuse me" turned towards an elegant car and drove away.

At the end of the trial I was frightened; every person in the street looked like Szawacki the murderer to me. I wanted to leave Frankfurt as soon as possible, I feared for my life there. It was a difficult experience for me that I shall never forget.

Outside in the hall my nephew, Jopie, the son of my sister Pola, was waiting for me. I didn't know that he was there. He was the only one who was waiting for me. He was worried about me, he was afraid that perhaps I would break down inside the courtroom, and said to me: "Aunty, I don't know how you can confront him in this way." I answered: "Only I can know how much I held back in order to keep my self-control, had I known that you were outside, perhaps I would have broken down."

Later when I lay in my bed that night, I said to myself: Indeed, now I can clearly see my block, I can see all the camp, everything exactly as it was. How, is it that I couldn't point out every detail on the map? I was unable to concentrate. I saw the people who sat around the presidency table in front of me, and who spoke to me. Who were the judges? And who were all his defence attorneys? I thought to myself... All of them are criminals; all of them should face trial. Their ages were between 60-65, which means that when the war broke out, they all served in Hitler's army and now they were pursuing justice. No wonder this is what their trials looked like, when they have judges who were once their brothers in arms...

It turned out that after our liberation from the camps Szawacki had "spent" ten years in a Russian jail. When he was released, he returned to Germany. To my regret, after the trial he was released, as thirty years had passed since the war and he received amnesty.

My husband had said to me: "Carla, take care of yourself and think carefully about what it is you are going to do." I have to admit that ever since that testimony, which I gave in the court in Frankfurt, my health deteriorated.

When I watched the film about the expelling of the Jews of Holland on television, on Holocaust Remembrance Day, knowing that no one from the first transport returned except for me, I felt horribly sad. I recognised a woman in the film and even noticed the number on her arm, and I wondered: Where am I? Am I still there, or is this just a dream? That was the reason I decided to testify against Szawacki; it was a sacred task. I thought that I had to present myself there on behalf of the Dutch people as well, and believed that the Dutch government supported me.

When they showed where we had lived in the camps on television, including the boards and everything, all the tragic scenes came back to me and reopened all my old wounds. Consequently, I presented myself at "Yad Vashem" and gave my testimony about that period. That was my obligation to the coming generations, to make sure that the documentation of the pain and suffering of the Jews during the time of the holocaust would remain.

[Our aunt Carla passed away in 1990 at the age of 76].

Ida: At the end of the war Anton and I arrived in Amsterdam and built our home there. I gave birth to a daughter in 1946 and we named her Salka Gustava. Anton opened a ladies garment factory and we lived comfortably. Salka immigrated to Israel at a young age and in 1983 Anton and I followed her.

[During the same year, Anton drowned on Tel Aviv beach. Our aunt Ida passed away in 1990 at the age of 80.]

Jopie: I came out of the holocaust an orphan. I left Holland in 1947, and reached Israel in 1948, the year of the War of Independence. In Israel I was reunited with my Uncle Yaakov, whom I remembered well since he used to spoil me during my visit as a child to Skulsk. Uncle Yaakov loved me very much, any time that I came to visit him in Haifa he used to take me to the fire brigade station where he worked and to the orchestra in which he played. I had the privilege of being among the family members who had survived the holocaust and I participated in his marriage ceremony to my Aunt Yael.

A big group of youngsters from the port of Haifa, including myself, were sent to the "Ahava" institution that belonged to the "Youth Aliyah" in Kiryat Bialik, I was then under sixteen. I stayed in the institution until the age of eighteen. As a youngster, just sixteen years old, I was already a "soldier" in the "Gadna" [the Youth Battalions], protecting the place from the Arabs of Shfar'am. At the age of eighteen I was drafted to the "Nahal" [the Pioneers Combatant Youth] and I did my basic training in "Camp 80". I was sent to a "Moshav" [cooperative Israeli settlement] called Moledet, by which time I was a trained soldier. A group of young men from there got together in order to establish a settlement by the name of Ramot Yair. That was where I met someone from kibbutz Tsuba and followed him there.

David Lewenhoff, Aunt Carla's husband, who was in Israel on a visit, came to kibbutz Tsuba. He told me that he had been a good friend of my father's and was therefore worried about me and wished that I would return to Holland.

Consequently, I returned to Holland in the 1950's to study. Uncle David Lewenhoff knew that a plant for the production of flax and wool was going to be built in Israel and he wanted me to learn the profession. I studied for a few years and received a certificate.

Right to left: Standing: Jopie, Carlos, Hanna, Anton, Ida and Salka. Sitting: David, Carla, Yitshak and Menno

When I returned to Israel, I lived in Rehovot and worked in a factory in Kiryat Mal'achi as a production manager. While living in Rehovot I was introduced to Aliza Shternberg and in 1957 we got married. I sent Sar-Louis an invitation to the wedding and then he finally understood that my father's wish had come true, and that I really was going to live my life in Israel.

Aliza graduated from nursing school and worked for years as a nurse in the public health sector, except for the years when we were serving abroad, when she worked at the embassy.

After a few years of working at the flax factory, I decided to complete my education. I finished my basic studies, and went on to study at university in Amsterdam. In the meantime, our first son, Avi, was born in Israel. We travelled to Amsterdam and lived there for nine years and our second son, Eyal, was born there in 1964. We later returned to live in Israel. I worked at "El Al" and in the Prime Minister's Office, and in between we went abroad on a few missions.

My son Avi is called after my father **Avraham Yehudah**. He lives near us in Rehovot and works at a government office.

My son Eyal is also called after my father **Avraham Yehudah**

Landau. He lives with his wife Limor in the States and they have three daughters: Naama-Shulamit, Tamar and Hagar-Sara.

Aliza and I live in Rehovot; we have been married for fifty-five years and hope to live a long life in good health.

In 1961, Anton's father, the Dutch boy who helped me when I hid in the attic in Holland, came to visit us in Israel. From our point of view, he was a very dear guest. My son Avi who was still young then, called him "Opa" (grandfather in Dutch).

Lyia, the daughter of my uncle Pinhas, survived and after the war she decided to settle in Holland. She met a man who was older than her and a Christian; she married him and converted to Christianity since she wanted to detach herself from the "burden" of Judaism. She has four sons.

Roza, Lyia's sister also survived, got married and for a certain period lived with her sister, she later moved to South Africa.

Yukev: After the war I returned to Sompolno. I met Rela there for the first time and I took a liking to her. We travelled to Munich and got married there, and that was where our first son Alex was born. In 1948 we moved to Uruguay and our second son, Enrique, was born there. We opened a butcher's shop that provided well for us. Alex and Enrique immigrated to Israel and in 1971 and we followed them. [Yukev passed away in 2001 at the age of 88].

Yukev and Rela on their wedding day

The Closing of a Circle

Dovit: As fate would have it Hilik Bar, the first-born son of my sister Tova, is in public office. He is a Member of the Knesset, and the Deputy Speaker of the Knesset in Israel. Among his duties he was also nominated to be in charge of the inter-parliamentary relations between Israel and Poland.

The Foreign Minister of Poland, Grzegorz Schetyna, came to visit the Knesset and Hilik hosted him. The Minister invited Hilik for a reciprocal visit in Warsaw. Hilik responded positively, but requested that he should leave one day free in his schedule so that he could visit Skulsk, the town were his grandfather was born and grew up. The Polish Foreign Minister was taken by surprise.

Hilik arrived in Skulsk in August 2015 and was respectfully received. During his visit, he was surprised to hear stories about the family from local people who still remembered the Kotowski family. He was presented with pictures of the family, a short film of Hanna giving testimony and even with documents from the town archives, signed by his great grandfather Itcze Kotowski. Hilik also inaugurated a memorial stone at the entrance to the old Jewish cemetery, which had been covered by soil and grass for many years. It was amazing, very moving and not something that one can take for granted.

It turned out that there was a Polish teacher, native of Skulsk, called Doctor Andrzej Kujawski, who had researched the history of the Kotowski family in depth, since he had a direct link to the story.

His mother's first husband, Jan Ciszewski, had gone to war together with my father, but did not return; his body was never found and he was considered missing. My father knew this and used his name, Jan Ciszewski, when he forged his identity documents in Jozefow.

After Hilik's visit, a visit for all the descendants of the Kotowski family was organised. Some of us had doubts and reservations, but eventually sixteen members of the family came to Skulsk over Passover 2016, among us grandsons and great grandsons of Itcze and Gitel Kotowski. In addition, one of the Gabrisz Rogorzynski's sons, Hannan Keren, and his wife Malca, plus a cousin of Gabrisz's and her daughter, also came.

We were received with respect and a number of ceremonies were held for us; we said Kaddish and "Yizkor" [a memorial prayer] at the old Jewish cemetery of Skulsk, where Aharon Leib is buried. A few years after the end of the war, in the 1950's, the

Kotowski family's stone house was completely burnt down and was no longer fit for living in. Later the two family houses and the two warehouses that had stood in the yard were also destroyed, and the Town Hall of "Gmina" Skulsk was built on the family's private land instead. The foundations of the New Town Hall stand on top of the foundations of the stone house that was built for Aharon. The central square of Skulsk today, stands where the yard of our family's house had been, and where every morning the commerce in building materials had taken place. During our visit, further to a decision taken by the council of the town, the square received a new name and it is now called: "The Kotowski Family Square".

Today two memorial stones with engraved metal plaques on them commemorate the liquidated Skulsk Jewish community, one at the entrance to the old Jewish cemetery and the other at "The Kotowski Family Square".

On the plaques the following is engraved in Hebrew, Polish and English:

"Remember what the Amalekite did to you,

In memory of the Jewish Community of Skulsk, that lived here and contributed to Skulsk's culture and arts and to its commerce and trade, until it was almost completely annihilated in the Holocaust by the Nazis and their helpers.

This memorial stone was inaugurated on 10th August 2015, in the presence of the Deputy Speaker of the Knesset, MK Yehiel (Hilik) Bar, great grandson of the late Gitel and Yitzhak Kotowski, who was the leader of Skulsk's Jewish Community"

On the following day we were taken on a sightseeing tour of the town. We saw and walked down the path that goes from the house's yard to the lake; we saw the lake, or what my father used to call the Ye'or, and told me about so many times. We walked along the streets where all the houses that had once belonged to the Jews of Skulsk were; some of them belonging to relatives and friends of the family. We passed by the place where the synagogue that had been destroyed once stood, and of which no remnant was left today. We saw the firemen's building and the church on the hill; and our emotions soared.

We visited Sompolno, including the town's synagogue that had somehow not been destroyed; it was recently renovated and is used today as the town's library, and in its yard, there are remnants of gravestones from the destroyed Jewish cemetery. While we were there we discussed and thought about the fact that in this very place, on festivals, and the Sabbath, and even on ordinary days, our relatives from the Wilczynski family had prayed. The mayor of Sompolno took me and Shahar, the grandson of Ida and Anton Piotrowski, to the house where Anton was born and grew up, and it was very moving.

After a year, on 9th July 2017, Efri and I travelled to Poland again. This time we went to Jozefow Bilgorajski, in order to take part in the ceremony to commemorate the 75th anniversary of the biggest and final massacre in Jozefow. The ceremony took place on 13th July 2017. We reached Poland a few days before the ceremony and stayed in a Hotel in Bilgoraj, from which we travelled to the surrounding towns and villages, following in the footsteps of my father Yaakov, his sister Hanna and his brother Yehudah.

In Bilgoraj we met Artur Bara who is a Polish Christian and a member of the City Council of Bilgoraj. Artur is a close friend of Israel Bar-On's, who is the Chairman of the "Descendants of Bilgoraj Society" in Israel. Israel and Artur are both active together in the preservation and commemoration of the Jews of Bilgoraj in Poland. Israel and Efri are childhood friends from the time that they both played in the Gadna Symphony Orchestra and participated in the orchestra's concert tours around the world.

Artur, a charming person, accompanied us over the five days of our visit to Bilgoraj and its surroundings. Artur arranged all the meetings with the mayors of the towns that we wanted to meet; he was also concurrently our translator and our tour guide.

On the first day we travelled to Hrubieszow and met there with the mayor, Ian Molodecki, and his senior assistant, who tried to answer our questions. They explained to us that Dembinka, the place where Yehudah was shot, is a forest close to Hrubieszow, and they assumed according to our stories that the Germans had had a detention camp there, where they probably executed anybody that they considered as their enemy. They could not confirm this with certainty though.

From Hrubieszow we travelled on to Husynne, a small, beautiful and serene village where Yehudah had lived and worked till he was caught and murdered. On our way to Husynne we could see the forest of Dembinka from a distance.

We travelled to Cichoborz, the village were my father had lived and served as a spy until the Poles informed on him. My aunt Hanna also lived there for about a year. We met with the head of the village who introduced us to an old local couple, 86 years of age. To our regret none of the people whom we met there could further enrich our knowledge.

On the second day we travelled to the killing pits in Jozefow. We walked around in the forest and saw the fenced pits, which are now covered by vegetation and trees. When you look inside the pits and try to imagine what exactly happened there seventy-five years ago, the mind is unable to comprehend it and the soul is unable to bear it. Our grandmother Gitel Kotowski is buried in one of these pits.

We held a private ceremony here. I read from the words of my father and my aunt Hanna, about the terrible things that had taken place there, and I sang the song "On the Day of Their Death", which my father had written and Liron Avioz, my student, composed music to. It was a beautiful day, the sky was blue, the sun was shining and the forest stood silent. Only the birds' singing could be heard around us, exactly as my father had described in his song. These were very emotional moments. Even Artur who does not know any Hebrew was moved.

We visited the local synagogue that has been reconstructed and is currently used as the municipal library. On our way back we passed the railway station which is situated a few kilometres from Jozefow. We assume that this was the station at which the Jews of Konin, and the surrounding villages, arrived on 22nd February 1941, and from which they reached the town of Jozefow.

The ceremony to commemorate the 75th anniversary of the great massacre in Jozefow took place on the fourth day. It was the most emotional day of the trip. All the days of our trip had been beautiful and sunny, but this day was characterised by a gloomy sky and non-stop rain; even the heavens cried. Roman Dziura, the Mayor of Jozefow, who arrived accompanied by his deputy and a number of Polish policemen from Jozefow, gave an address. After him Yossi Avni, whose family had been from Jozefow, and most of whom had perished there, spoke. Efri spoke after him, describing how the train that had departed from Lodz had arrived in Jozefow, inside it 1,300 Jews that had been deported from Konin and the surrounding towns.

He described some of what the passengers had gone through on the way and cited the song "On the Day of Their Death" in English; then Artur read it in Polish and I played the song that my student Liron Avioz had performed in Hebrew. After that, Markus Feibiger, the head of the Police Academy of Hamburg, gave an address, a Polish priest said a prayer in memory of the murdered people, Efri said Kaddish and finally, flower wreathes were laid on the monument. The Germans bowed their heads in front of the memorial and laid a giant flower wreath of red roses on it. After the ceremony we were all invited to a meal by the mayor of Jozefow.

After the meal I sat with the head of the German delegation of Hamburg's police and his aids, and told them the story of our family. He listened attentively and seemed shocked by parts of the story.

We returned to Bilgoraj and the sky cleared as if it had not rained at all that day.

On the following morning we travelled back to Warsaw. On the way we stopped at the extermination camp of Majdanek and saw the Jews' living and working barracks, the gas chambers and the crematoria. This visit too was very emotional, since Majdanek is where our grandfather, Itcze Kotowski, may he rest in peace, perished. Being there was very difficult since the mind cannot fathom what we know happened there, and it is very difficult for the soul to comprehend it. Here too we led a private ceremony, in which we also played an especially moving version of the prayer for the dead, "El Male Rahamim" [O God, Full of Compassion], performed by the chief cantor of the I.D.F, Shai Abramson.

It was Friday evening when we reached Warsaw. We went to "Chabad House", for Kiddush and the Shabbat meal. After such a difficult and emotional journey, to sit around a table for Shabbat Kiddush in Poland and sing Shabbat Songs, among others "Am Israel Chai" ["the people of Israel live on…"], had a special and exhilarating meaning.

And this was the closing of a circle for us; an end to the fascinating survival story of the Kotowski family.

What I personally learnt from this experience was the following: It is better to live in a modest house in my homeland than in a golden palace in the Diaspora.

History repeats itself over and over again. In every generation there are those who will want to annihilate us and the only variable is the enemy. Anti-Semitism hasn't disappeared from the world, regrettably it is becoming stronger, as are its accompanying dangers; the difference is that today we have a State and a strong army. If any enemy rises up against us with the intent of annihilating us, we are able to fight back; in the hope that we may never have to.

The five survivors: Right to left: Carla, Hanna, Yaakov, Golda and Ida. Israel 15.08.1968

A Letter to my Father

My Dear Father,

I shall never forget how you brought me up with such love. I was your youngest daughter and you showered me with delights that my brother and sister could not have dreamt of receiving. All your life you were active and busy, you worked hard in shifts at the fire brigade, and you nurtured a big garden around the house; it had two chicken coops and turkeys too. You grew fruit and vegetables in the garden and it also had a decorative part. You took care of the dogs, Humi and Rexi, who guarded the yard. You cooked and served us healthy meals at a time when there was no awareness regarding these things yet. You kept the house clean both inside and out. On Friday nights you made Kiddush for us and at the festivals you made us festive meals, following all the blessings so we would learn all the traditions.

When I was small you took me by bicycle to kindergarten and later to school, you sang me songs and told me stories. You helped me shower in the summer and drew me baths in the winter; you took me to the beach and took care that I, being a red-head, would not God forbid get burnt by the sun. You helped me do my homework in Hebrew and arithmetic, and you gave me tips on how not to get confused between "aleph" (the first letter in the Hebrew alphabet) and "ayin" (the sixteenth letter in the Hebrew alphabet). You sat next to me by the piano, corrected my mistakes and tried to teach me how to play the music with feeling. You made sure that I always had plenty of chocolate and cookies at hand. You did everything with devotion and patience. You said that, except for breast-feeding us you did everything to nurture us, and you were right.

You lived modestly, you spared everything from yourself, but you didn't spare a thing from us, you gave us as much as you could. In spite of the great pain that you carried in your heart throughout your life, when you stood on the kitchen porch cleaning the fish or pluck-ing a chicken, you sang softly and sometimes whistled a cheerful tune. You always had a smile on your face; you were cheerful and ready to hear a good joke. You liked to laugh, to joke, you told jokes and believed that in the end everything would turn out fine, an op-timist from birth. You always finished anything you wrote in this tone: "Tonight let's be happy and rejoice, and let it be with Mazal Tov (good fortune); Let us raise a glass to the heavens and hopefully achieve peace soon";

and you used a lot of rhyme in your writings.

Once in a while you told us about what you had experienced in the past, about the beautiful life that you had had before the war and about the sequence of events during the war. You cried for your mother and father, for Pola and her family and for Aharon Leib. You also cried when you told us how they had killed small Zefirka, and Rozboj, your terrifying and loyal dog; and there was no limit to your pain when you told us about Yehudah, who you loved with all your heart and soul, and you claimed that your life was redeemed by his.

When you told us about the war you told us about how you fell into captivity, how Yukev saved you, that you returned home, and that you were then expelled from here to there, that you worked hard labour in horrible conditions, how you ran away from place to place, how you were saved when the war was over. Everything was sterile, without any shocking stories, and I, in my naivety, thought that you were spared all these terrible things. But one day I visited Aunt Hanna and I asked her to tell me some stories from the past. Aunt Hanna gave me the testimony that she had written at the end of the war in Holland to read. I cannot recall having ever read any document so fast. From the moment that I started to read the testimony and until I finished it I didn't take my eyes off it. I felt my breath leave me, I was paralyzed, I was in shock. Only then did I realise that you had never mentioned the horrible things that had happened to you. I understood that you wanted to protect me, so that I wouldn't feel pain, that you wanted to spare me from all this, so that I would not suffer, since the stories were impossible to digest.

You came from a religious house; your father was a Hassid of the Rabbi of Gur. You said that after the war you stopped believing and that if mother had not kept the traditions going at home, you would have given them up too. In spite of all this you still liked the scriptures; you always kept the "Siddur" [Jewish prayer book] and the Bible by your head, and when you went to sleep or rest, you would always first read from them. Your language was spiced with expressions from the Bible, sayings and proverbs of the sages of the Mishna and the Talmud, full of idiomatic phrases. You liked to write in their language, but you changed the sources to meet your needs, according to what you felt. When my friends came to visit me, you would bless them in this language and they would always laugh. That is part of the legacy that you left us and I have tried to integrate it into the book in which I relate our family's history.

You loved mother so much, she was your entire world. Mother was beautiful, gentle, pleasant and educated. You always told us that when you met her she had many suitors and that they "stuck to her like flies". You were proud of how only you succeeded in "getting rid of" them. Every Shabbat morning you served mother tea and a piece of cake while she was still in bed. Later you brought her to the

254 | Scattered Rays of Light

kitchen, where we, the children sat and ate the breakfast that you had prepared for us, while she was still in her pyjamas; you hugged and kissed her and called her pet names like "Chochka". When a waltz was played on the radio and mother was at home, you invited her to dance; you would dance with each other, just like that in the middle of the day, in the middle of life, with no special reason. Today I know that mother was your tranquilliser.

When mother got sick you took care of her with endless devotion; you rushed with her to doctors and took care of all her needs, and when she had no strength left, you washed her like one wash a baby. When mother passed away, I felt as if you were going through another Shoah; you didn't stop crying.

And today, when I look at the few photos that I have from your wedding day with mother, the day that should have been the happiest day of your life, it is impossible not to see the sad look in your eyes. On this happiest of days everyone is accompanied by their closest and dearest relatives. But on your wedding day, where were your mother and father? Where were Pola, Avraham and little Shulamit? Aharon and your dear brother Yehuda, and all your aunts, uncles and numerous cousins from Skulsk and Sompolno...? I believe that they were all hovering above you and participating in your day of joy. There, from above, they organised a feast fit for a king for you, just like the one that Pola and Avraham had back in the good days before the war.

In April 2016 I travelled with Tova, Efri and the children to Poland, to Skulsk. "We were like dreamers", meaning, it was such a wonderful and special experience for me that it is impossible to compare it to what we usually see, but more like a wonderful dream. I felt like I was floating on air, as if I was touched by you and the entire heritage that you left us. I could not believe that this was real. Was it possible that I had reached Skulsk; that I was treading on the soil where you were born and had grown up? Is it possible that today, seventy five years after the war, young Poles are learning about and know of the existence of the magnificent Jewish community that was once there and doesn't exist anymore? Is it possible that there are residents in the town that still remember the Kotowski family? I felt so happy, and I believe that you too were watching over everything that happened there from above.

I shall carry your pain in my heart till the day that I die. Although I gave you a lot of attention, I shall suffer the thought; perhaps I didn't give you the full attention that you deserved? Today I know that you deserved much more. I vowed that I shall fulfil the commandment "Remember what the Amalekite did to you", with all my heart, the same commandment that your father gave you before he was led to the fiery furnace in the extermination camp of Majdanek. You fulfilled his commandment meticulously; before any event, sad or happy, you took the pains, wrote and read from your writings; when you stood in front of the gravestone in memory of those who had perished from Konin and the surrounding area, at our weddings, when our children were born and on the eve of any festival, you took the trouble to remember and to remind us. I shall pass on this book that I painstakingly wrote, together with Efri, over endless days and nights, in a constant flood of tears, to the future generations.

And finally, as my brother Efri says: "You were the bravest of the brave, the most daring among the daring. Like our forefather Jacob, who wrestled with the angel on the Ford of the Jabbok stream all night until the break of day and prevailed, you too wrestled with the angel of death, with great force, looked him straight in the eye, and you prevailed.

Like the Phoenix, the legendary sand fowl who rose from his own ashes, you rose, and from the ashes of Majdanek you sprouted new branches, creating a family that became a large tribe, one that you can take pride in."

Your soul dwells and will dwell here with us for ever. I am sure that it and the souls of all your loved ones dwell in peace in the Garden of Eden. May your soul be bound up in the bond of everlasting life.

Your daughter, that will love you forever,
Dovit.

Bibliography

The written testimonies of our late aunt Hanna Kotowski Krzywanowski Gonsiorowicz.

The written testimony of our late aunt Carla Kotowski Lewenhoff Marchak.

The written testimonies of our late father Yaakov Eliezer Kotowski Pedatsur and the stories that we heard from him in our childhood.

The testimony of our cousin Yoseph (Jopie) Landau.

The booklet "The Wilczynski Saga" published in 2003 and edited by our sister Tova and our cousins, Jo-Beth and Shmuel Roney Ben Yehudah and Valeria and Menno Krzywanowski.

The booklet "Our Life's Story", edited by our father's late cousin Yukev Wilczynski and his wife Rela.

The booklet "A Package of Memories", edited by our father's late cousin, Moshe Biderko.

The booklet written in memory of our family's childhood friend, the late Gabrisz Rogorzynski.

Documents that were discovered and stories that were heard by our nephew Hilik Bar during his visit to Skulsk in 2015.

The testimony of Zigmunt Nasielski, which Efri heard during his visit to Skulsk in 2003.

Information received from Dr Andrzej Kujawski, PhD, a Polish teacher native of Skulsk, during our visit there in 2016. Wikipedia

Made in the USA
Coppell, TX
10 February 2022

73339084R00144